victory

restorat...

...for

...veness

healing

joy

power

giveness

healing

joy

victory

restoration

To:

From:

© 2013 by Matthew West

All rights reserved. No portion of this book may be reproduced, stored in a retrieval system, or transmitted in any form or by any means—electronic, mechanical, photocopy, recording, scanning, or other—except for brief quotations in critical reviews or articles, without the prior written permission of the publisher.

Published in Nashville, Tennessee, by Thomas Nelson. Thomas Nelson is a registered trademark of Thomas Nelson, Inc.

Published in association with the literary agency of Fedd and Company, Inc., PO Box 341973, Austin, Texas 78734.

Cover design by Mary Hooper at Milkglass Creative.

Thomas Nelson, Inc., titles may be purchased in bulk for educational, business, fund-raising, or sales promotional use. For information, please e-mail SpecialMarkets@ThomasNelson.com.

Unless otherwise indicated, all Scripture quotations are taken from the *Holy Bible*, New Living Translation, © 1996, 2004, 2007 by Tyndale House Foundation. Used by permission of Tyndale House Publishers, Inc., Carol Stream, Illinois 60188. All rights reserved.

Scripture quotations marked NIV are taken from the Holy Bible, New International Version®. Copyright © 1973, 1978, 1984, 2011 by Biblica, Inc.™ Used by permission of Zondervan. All rights reserved worldwide. www.zondervan.com

Scripture quotations marked NKJV are taken from the NEW KING JAMES VERSION. © 1982 by Thomas Nelson, Inc. Used by permission. All rights reserved.

Scripture quotations marked ESV are taken from the ENGLISH STANDARD VERSION. © 2001 by Crossway Bibles, a division of Good News Publishers. Used by permission.

Scripture quotations marked GW are taken from God's Word, a copyrighted work of God's Word to the Nations. Copyright © 1995 by God's Word to the Nations. All rights reserved. Used by permission.

ISBN-13: 978-1-4003-2256-5

Printed in Mexico

13 14 15 16 RRD 7 6 5 4

FORGIVENESS

MATTHEW WEST

COUNTRYMAN ®

A Division of Thomas Nelson Publishers
Since 1798

THOMAS NELSON ®
Since 1798

NASHVILLE   DALLAS   MEXICO CITY   RIO DE JANEIRO

CONTENTS

FORGIVING YOURSELF

EMBRACING GOD'S FORGIVENESS

FOREWORD

I remember the moment like it was yesterday.

Donald and I were newly married, new believers, on fire for all things God. We loved being at church, whether in the service or teaching Sunday School or hanging out with our Bible study group. That week we welcomed someone new to our apartment where we hosted the Wednesday night meeting.

Her name was Kathy Landers and she came alone.

Just her and her well-worn Bible.

Kathy was in her late forties, blonde with a pretty smile. But that wasn't what we noticed first about her. First we noticed Kathy's peace. A crazy, wildly encompassing peace that walked with her through our front door and sat beside her on the sofa through coffee and introductions.

A peace that filled the room.

We asked Kathy to share her story. She sat a little straighter and her eyes lit up. "I was married for twenty-one years to the love of my life, the greatest man I ever knew. His name was Tom." Her eyes sparkled like a love-struck teenager. "We did everything together and we shared a very deep faith in God." She went on, her pace unrushed. She and Tom had married young and together raised two children—a boy and a girl.

The longer Kathy talked about Tom, the more uneasy I felt. Why was she speaking in the past tense? I braced myself for whatever was coming.

Kathy paused and caught her breath. A hint of sadness colored her expression. "One year ago Tom was shot and killed by one of his work friends. I figured it was time I get back to a Bible study." Her smile came from somewhere deep inside her. "So here I am."

Silence followed. Finally someone asked what happened and Kathy told us. A year ago her husband had gone duck hunting with a buddy from work. The guy knew nothing about guns, but he wanted to learn. The idea seemed fun so the two planned an all-day trip. "I remember the morning Tom left. None of us had any idea what was coming."

Tom and his friend headed out to a remote lake. The morning went well, with Tom teaching the guy how to aim and shoot at the ducks. But Tom's friend didn't get any solid shots at the ducks. Just after noon, the buddy began finding more enjoyment shooting other targets.

That's when the tragedy happened.

Tom's friend suddenly turned the gun away from the target and aimed it at Tom. "We should play paintball sometime . . ."

Before he finished his sentence, he accidentally pulled the trigger. Tom was shot in the head and died within minutes. Kathy had tears in her eyes as she told the story. "It was an accident, of course. Later, Tom's friend would tell police he thought the gun was empty." She paused. "He also told them that Tom had clearly said to never point a gun at a person. The guy said he just wasn't thinking."

No charges were pressed against the friend, and the guy was able to move on with his life. As I listened, frustration seethed inside me. I had a special level of anger in my heart for people who were so clearly careless. But my rage didn't stand a chance against my curiosity.

"How can you have such peace?" I looked at her, trying to understand. "I would think you'd be angry. I mean, it wasn't fair, what happened."

"No, it wasn't." Tears filled her eyes, even while her content-edness remained. "Our kids lost their father. I lost the only man

I'll ever love." She nodded slowly. "I tried being bitter and angry. I almost lost myself."

She explained that God had shown her a better way. "I woke up one morning and I knew I had to forgive him. Either that or I'd die in my bitterness—an angry woman my precious Tom wouldn't have recognized."

What did Kathy do?

She met up with Tom's buddy for lunch one day and gave him a Bible. "I looked him in the eyes and took hold of his hands. We'd never met, so I told him who I was and that I had forgiven him." Her smile came easily at that part of the story. "He's a Christian now. We write to each other every now and then." For a long time she waited, gathering her emotions. "I miss Tom every day of my life. But I have peace. Only forgiveness can do that."

Kathy's story changed the way I look at the idea of forgiveness. If God can forgive me . . . if Kathy could forgive the man who shot and killed her husband . . . then I can forgive others. I was so struck by Kathy's story I used it as the basis of one of my first novels, *Waiting for Morning*. The subject of the book is the same as the one you are holding right now.

Forgiveness.

As Matthew West sings in his life-changing song, "The prisoner that you really free is you."

The keys are in this book.

—Karen Kingsbury

#1 *New York Times* bestselling author Karen Kingsbury is America's favorite inspirational storyteller, with more than twenty million copies of her award-winning books in print. Her latest novel, *The Chance*, also deals with forgiveness. Karen and Matthew are friends and have appeared at events together. Karen often writes her Life-Changing Fiction™ while listening to Matthew's music. She lives in Nashville, TN., with her husband, Don and their five almost grown sons, three of whom were adopted from Haiti. Their daughter, Kelsey, appeared in Matthew West's *The Heart of Christmas* movie. She is married to Christian recording artist Kyle Kupecky.

INTRODUCTION

I need this book. And, since you're reading it, I have a feeling you might need this book as well. Truth is, at some point in life, all of us will wind up having to figure out what to do about forgiveness. On any given day, in any given situation, involving any given relationship, we may find ourselves forced to face the complexities of forgiveness from a number of vantage points. Actually, we begin receiving an education on forgiveness early in life. As children, we may not be able to define or completely understand the full meaning of the word, but we can see the need for forgiveness on any school playground or during any family vacation. In fact, "I'm sorry" is one of the first things kids are taught to include in their budding vocabulary. I'll give you an example.

Snapshots from Home

For the most part, Lulu and Delaney get along. But like all sisters, they do have their moments of discord when peace and harmony give way to bickering and blaming. When you're dealing with a seven-year-old and a four-year-old, it's bound to happen. The reason I know so much about these little girls is because they are mine. As their dad I have had to learn how to navigate the often unpredictable drama that arises between two sassy sisters.

Thankfully, I myself had some good teaching in this area when, many years ago, my parents were charged with a similar task. Only instead of little girls, they were blessed with boys, and I'm the oldest. How do I put this nicely? On occasion, my brothers and I failed to see eye to eye. Oh, who am I kidding? Some days we fought like cats and dogs. *Most* days we fought like pro wrestlers in a steel-cage death match!

My parents developed some pretty disarming tactics that always seemed to have a way of defusing a moment of tension and enabling us to settle our differences by the time all was said and done. Their extensive arsenal of conflict resolution tactics included the ever popular and never-out-of-style time-out.

This forced my brothers and me to separate, cool off, and take some time to think a bit more rationally . . . before resuming our cage match.

Another approach my parents implemented when we were on family vacations was what I called the "Invisible Line." We would pile into our old, red Ford station wagon, and tension would rise with the summer temperatures as we racked up the highway miles. I remember my dad pulling the car over to the side of the interstate on more than one occasion. He would turn around to face us and draw an invisible line down the middle of the backseat. Then he handed down an unthinkable consequence that worked every time: "If either of you crosses this line, then when we get to Disney World, instead of going into the park, you will have to take a nap." Cruel, cruel punishment. But you better believe I didn't cross that line again!

One of the most memorable and effective strategies that the masterminds otherwise known as "Mom" and "Dad" liked to use involved hugging. Boys aren't huggers; boys are hitters. But from the beginning our parents set out to change that. As I write this, I have a mental picture of my middle brother and me making a beeline to my mother, trying to tell on each other and making sure we got our side of the story in first. "Mom, Matthew hit me on the arm!" "But he stole my baseball card!" My mother would listen to each of us whine our way through some lengthy explanation of why we were the wronged party, and then we would wait for her to hand down her judgment of who was right.

On more than one occasion, hugging was Mom's go-to response—and it would drive us nuts! "Boys, I want you to stand and face each other." We would turn to each other, but refuse to look the other in the eye. "Now, look each other in the eye." Reluctantly, with steam still pouring out of our ears, we would angrily make eye contact. "Now I want each of you to say you're sorry." "But Mom! Why should I . . ." "I don't want to hear it," she would interject. "Both of you say you're sorry." Each of us would then mumble our way through a halfhearted apology to get Mom off our backs. But she wasn't finished yet. Here came the clincher.

"Now," she said, "I want you to hug each other for ten seconds without letting go." NOOOOO!!!! I could handle facing my brother. I could even stomach looking the stealer of my baseball card in the eye for a couple seconds. But a hug? You've got to be kidding me! But we could tell Mom meant business. So, with what I am sure resembled two opposite ends of a magnet being pushed together, two brothers embraced for ten whole seconds!

I'm pretty sure we both held our breath that entire time as well. And the result?

Well, more often than not, we would find ourselves laughing at the sheer ridiculousness of this seemingly eternal hug. Somehow our grudge gave way to forgiveness and the reminder that, at the end of the day, we weren't enemies. We were brothers.

Now that I'm an adult, I wish I could say that forgiveness has become less of a hurdle over which I stumble, but the opposite is true. I find that forgiveness—both the receiving and the giving—goes against everything I think and feel and know to be fair and just and right. It just doesn't come naturally to me. Philip Yancey's words affirm that I'm not the only one: "I never find forgiveness easy, and rarely do I find it completely satisfying. Nagging injustices remain, and the wounds still cause pain. I have to approach God again and again, yielding to him the residue of what I thought I had committed to him long ago."[1]

Stories of Forgiveness

Over the past few years I have been on a mission to discover the power of the story that lies within all of us. I have collected well over twenty thousand true stories from people all across the United States and even twenty countries around the world. Men, women, teenagers, and even kids have told me their tales. People from all walks of life, backgrounds, and experiences have written to me, opening a window to their world and inviting me to look inside. These stories have further shown me that forgiveness is both an unavoidable part of life and an essential factor in finding peace, joy, and fulfillment as we live out our story. Reading these stories has also revealed four life-defining questions regarding forgiveness:

1. Is there someone in my life I need to forgive?
2. Is there someone I have wronged and need to ask to forgive me?
3. Have I forgiven myself for mistakes I've made in my past?
4. Have I embraced my need of the forgiveness God offers to me?

How we answer these questions will drastically affect our relationships with others, define our feelings about ourselves, and ultimately determine the course of our lives. Forgiveness can mean the difference between pain and joy, brokenness and

healing, confinement and freedom. Each of the stories I have selected for this book powerfully illustrate the importance of our responses to these four questions. The storytellers have opened a window to their world not just to me, but to you as well. When I first read their stories, I was drawn back to the Bible to rediscover the role forgiveness has played in people's life stories since the beginning of creation.

So my prayer is that, as you read these stories, both new and old, you will find yourself taking a good look at your own story. Consider this book a time-out for you, perhaps even as a long-overdue opportunity to examine your life, your relationships, your wounds, your past, your faith. I can almost guarantee that, like those ten-second hugs my brother and I shared, digging in to what God says about forgiveness will be uncomfortable at times. However, only the brave ones—only those of us willing to wrestle with this tough issue—will ever discover the joy, victory, healing, restoration, and power of one word: *forgiveness.*

> *Brothers, listen! We are here to proclaim that through this man Jesus there is forgiveness for your sins. Everyone who believes in him is declared right with God.*
>
> Acts 13:38-39

FORGIVING OTHERS

This section begins with a true story told by a woman named Renee. In fact, her story is actually the reason why this little book exists. A few years ago Renee was among the first to respond when I asked people to share their story. The moment I read her tragically beautiful telling of the freedom she found in forgiveness, I thought to myself, *The whole world needs to hear this story*. So here it is. . . .

It's the hardest thing to give away
The last thing on your mind today
It always goes to those who don't deserve

Forgiveness

RENEE

I never understood why God would ask Abraham to sacrifice Isaac, the son he had waited so long to have. I also always hoped He would never require such a sacrifice of me.

Once my first child, a son, was born, I *really* couldn't understand how Abraham just did what God told him to do. The love a parent has for a child is like no other. God also blessed me with three daughters, the last two being identical twins. I love my children with all my heart and could never imagine living without any one of them.

I now have a mission I did not choose: DUI presentations.

On May 11, 2002, a twenty-four-year-old drunk driver named Eric killed one of my twins, Meagan, and her friend Lisa, both girls twenty years old. This event was devastating for all three families involved and the countless friends who mourned the loss of these precious girls. Words cannot fully describe the pain and loss I felt.

In the weeks and months that followed, I spiraled into a

dark hole that I could not seem to get out of. Eric was the one behind bars, but I felt like the one being held prisoner. I could not imagine life without Meagan. I wanted to go back and fix it. But I couldn't do that.

I'd always had a childlike faith, but suddenly my faith had been shaken like never before. Everything I'd always believed in had been thrown up in the air, and I didn't know what to believe anymore. But I needed to know that there was a heaven. I wanted to believe my daughter was there and I would see her again. The grief was so heavy, I felt like it was going to suffocate me. I had no joy. I would listen to praise and worship music in my car, but I couldn't sing. I had so much anger inside of me, so much rage. But God wrapped His arms around me in that darkness. He let me know that He was with me.

I began to turn in the direction of forgiveness at Eric's sentencing, seventeen months after the accident. Throughout the entire trial Eric had shown little remorse for what he had done. This only served to fuel my anger. But I walked into his final sentencing already knowing in my heart I needed to forgive him. Then, as my entire family sat in the courtroom waiting to hear the judge's verdict, Eric stood to share some last words.

He began to weep as he said how sorry he was for what he had done. Then he turned to face my family and me. He stood there in handcuffs and a prison jumpsuit, tears streaming down his face, looking at me, and he said, "I would give my own life if it would bring back these girls, but it won't . . . and I'm so sorry."

That was a moment when healing began in my life. Suddenly, instead of anger, I began to feel compassion for this young man who had made a tragic mistake. For a long time I'd thought that by forgiving Eric, I would be betraying my daughter or, in a way, leaving her behind. I thought forgiving Eric was almost like saying, "What he did doesn't matter." But God showed me that forgiving Eric was the best way to honor Meagan and to assure that her loving legacy would live on.

Today my story is a story of healing and forgiveness. My family and Lisa's family chose to forgive Eric. We even appealed to have his twenty-two-year prison sentence reduced. The judge granted our request, and today Eric is a free man. But he's not the only one who is free. I've been set free from the burden I carried for so long, the burden of bitterness.

*To forgive is to set a prisoner free and then
discover that the prisoner was you.*

Lewis B. Smedes[1]

good story can make you lose yourself. A great one
can help you to find yourself too. A great story has the
power both to inspire you and trouble you. It can leave
you challenged but also conflicted. Renee's is a great story.

Usually I tend to work out my thoughts and emotions in response to stories like Renee's in my songwriting. But I humbly
admit that, as a songwriter, I hadn't the slightest clue how to give
her story a voice. How could I paint a delicate picture of a topic
that so many find so difficult? The main hurdle I couldn't seem to
get over was my fear that writing a song telling people they should
forgive would make me the greatest hypocrite in history: *How can
I write a song encouraging people to forgive like Renee has when I have a
hard enough time forgiving the guy who cuts me off in rush hour traffic,
let alone extending grace to someone who deeply offended me or—as in
Renee's case—took the life of someone I dearly loved? That kind of forgiveness seems impossible.* That's why the lyrics of the chorus wound up

being written as a prayer from a fool who struggles to forgive rather than as a command from an armchair quarterback:

> *Show me how to love the unlovable*
> *Show me how to reach the unreachable*
> *Help me now to do the impossible*
> *Forgiveness*

Those words stirred something in my soul, but the rest of the song remained unwritten. So I carried Renee's story around with me in my guitar case for a couple of years. Something just wouldn't allow the song to be finished, but I couldn't get Renee's story out of my head either. I now realize that God's perfect timing was the reason for the delay. Little did I know that very soon Eric would be released from prison. Since Renee had written to me, I had no idea how her story—and Eric's—had unfolded.

Out of curiosity, on the day I finished recording Renee's song, "Forgiveness," I did a Google search of her name to see if I could find any updates to her story. I sat in shock as I read in *The Huffington Post* of Eric's pending release from prison. Now I understood: the song that I had struggled to complete was not meant for two years ago; it was a song for such a time as this.

My heart leaped for joy upon the realization that Eric would be released from prison, a free man, just as their song would be playing on radio stations all across the country. This was shaping up to be a special season that God had undoubtedly orchestrated. Soon the world would have the chance to witness what I had seen a few years earlier through Renee's testimony: the power of forgiveness.

Looking back at the lyrics of the song, I clearly understood that God had His hand on my pen. I know of no other way to explain how surprisingly relevant lines like these are to Renee and Eric's story:

> *It'll clear the bitterness away*
> *It can even set a prisoner free*
> *There is no end to what its power can do*
> *So let it go and be amazed*
> *By what you see through eyes of grace*
> *The prisoner that it really frees is you*
> *Forgiveness*

When I originally penned those words, I had no idea that a prisoner was about to, literally, be set free. I was just so moved by Renee's discovery that she needed what forgiveness had to offer just as much as the offender did, saying, "Eric was the one behind bars, but I felt like the one being held prisoner." Author G. K. Chesterton wrote, "To love means loving the unlovable. To forgive means pardoning the unpardonable. Faith means believing the unbelievable. Hope means hoping when everything seems hopeless." Renee will be the first to tell you that forgiveness is anything but easy. But her story reveals the lesson she learned: forgiveness is a necessity.

Psalm 30:5 promises, "Weeping may last through the night, but joy comes with the morning." Renee has spent more nights weeping than any mother should. And because she will forever miss her daughter, Renee will most likely weep some more until the day she is once again reunited with her beloved Meagan. But just like Eric, Renee is no longer a prisoner. Forgiveness has set her free. Corrie ten Boom, the inspiring evangelist and author who suffered greatly under Hitler's regime and in his concentration camps, wrote this: "Forgiveness is the key that unlocks the door of resentment and the handcuffs of hatred. It is a power that breaks the chains of bitterness and the shackles of selfishness."[2]

If you weep with the groans of injustice or because of loss beyond words, take heart. Joy is coming. And forgiveness will help you recognize and receive it.

JOE

This happened a few years back. My wife and I, both believers, had been married for about twenty-three years when we started falling away from God, not fellowshipping, not reading the Bible, and not praying. Just generally falling away and, at the same time, becoming distant from each other. Kind of living our own separate lives. We weren't fighting or being nasty to each other. Just distant. Well, I ended up having an affair, and it lasted for months. Cheryl, my wife, suspected, but I kept denying. It finally came to a head. I admitted it and was set to leave her for this other woman.

Then a longtime friend—who is also a brother in the Lord—stepped in and talked to me. He happened to call right when I was packing some stuff up to leave. He didn't even know I was home. He called to check on Cheryl. He was about an hour away, but he promised to be at his house in an hour and wanted me to come and talk to him. At first I refused, but something made me decide to talk with him. When I did, he reminded me of where I had come from. How close to God I was for so long. He reminded me of a time he and I were driving along the road, and when we saw a nice view of some beautiful scenery, I'd said to him, "I know the Guy who made that!" My offhand comment had stuck with him. As we talked together, God softened my heart and called me back to Him.

I called the other woman and told her I was going back to my wife—and back to God. Then I called Cheryl and told her. When I got home, she was outside waiting for me, and we ran to each other's arms! Oh, man! What a moment! It brings tears to my eyes as I write this! That was almost eight years ago. Cheryl accepted me back, and we built our relationship back up by putting God at the forefront. We've never been happier, and for all the world, I would never ever give her up again!

This is what forgiveness means to me. It means that the love my wife has for me is so very real that, although I don't even deserve to have her ever be a part of my life, she has decided to put the hurts, the deception, the violation aside, to welcome me to be her husband, and to rebuild what we had lost. As I think about this forgiveness, I am overwhelmed. I am completely unworthy. I had sinned against my God, my wife, and myself. I had violated the vow I had made to my wife. Yet God forgives me and accepts me just as my wife forgives me and accepts me. I can't think about this without a flood of emotion washing over me. It thrills me beyond compare.

I think the one word I associate with forgiveness is *love*. True love. Real love. Overwhelming love. Undeserved love. The kind of love I almost destroyed. But God saw to it and restored love in our lives! He made it possible for us to renew our relationship with Him and with each other. Nothing else in my life comes close to this feeling of being forgiven and this truth that I am truly loved. Cheryl and I have experienced the hand of God, and He is very real to us! Now forgiveness is an ever-present truth in my life. I've lived it.

RESTORED

> *[God] has restored our relationship with him through Christ, and has given us this ministry of restoring relationships.*

2 Corinthians 5:18 GW

I have read hundreds of stories that center around the topic of marriage. I have read about the good, the bad, and the ugly. And I've read enough—and been married long enough—to know that every marriage will have its fair share of all three. Sadly, many of the stories I read have an ending I wish I had the power to rewrite. Vows broken, love betrayed, and one or both spouses choosing to go when the going got tough. Many marriages that are invaded by infidelity do end in divorce. Some endings are unavoidable: one spouse may have absolutely no desire to see a marriage through. But Joe's story testifies to the power of forgiveness and how God can miraculously mend a relationship that appears far beyond repair.

Joe's marriage had never been worse. He made a poor choice and walked away from the riches of God's blessing, the riches of marriage and a wife. Joe chose an unhealthy relationship with someone other than his wife, and he was on the verge of breaking every single vow he had made to her. He was about to leave before "death do us part." But this is where grace stepped in. The real hero in this story is Joe's wife, Cheryl. With God's help, she forgave her husband and made the bold choice to trust that God could somehow restore what the Enemy had all but destroyed.

As I write this, I realize that Cheryl's forgiveness story—like many I selected for this book—offers a picture of forgiveness that leaves me humbled by the thought, *I don't think I could forgive if I were in her situation.* I can't even bear the thought of finding out that my closest friend, my partner in life, my wife had been unfaithful. It makes me sick to my stomach just to think about it. Yet I am drawn to stories like these because they remind me just how lopsided forgiveness can feel, how forgiveness can go against any logic and every definition of what is fair in our eyes or in the eyes of the world.

When I am wronged, I want justice. When I am the one who was wrong, I prefer grace. But if the end result of forgiveness were fairness, grace would not be necessary. We would always get what we deserve, and no one would ever get a second chance. Grace is unmerited, undeserved, unearned, and unequal favor— and grace is anything but fair. Philip Yancey wrote, "Forgiveness offers a way out. It does not settle all questions of blame and fairness—often it pointedly evades those questions—but it does allow a relationship to start over, to begin anew."[3] Eight years after Cheryl forgave Joe, they stand together as proof that a relationship can start over.

Starting over has to start somewhere. Both Joe and Cheryl

could have chosen easier roads. Joe's bags were packed. He could have left, as many husbands do, making Cheryl's decision much easier. Or Cheryl could have kicked Joe to the curb and told him never to return again, making Joe feel that he was right to pack those bags after all. But in this story neither Cheryl nor Joe chose the easy road. Instead of pride, Joe chose humility. Instead of excuses, Joe chose repentance. Instead of hatred, Cheryl chose love. Instead of revenge, Cheryl chose mercy. Make no mistake about it: that picture Joe painted of the reunited couple hugging and crying in the driveway was only the first step on what has been a long road to restoration. And if either one had balked at the possibility of reconciliation, this story would have a much different ending. Lewis B. Smedes wrote, "It takes one person to forgive. It takes two people to be reunited."[4] Forgiveness in situations like these only happens for those who dare to believe that some things in life are worth fighting for. Joe and Cheryl fought for their marriage, and God is restoring it day by day.

Now, here's where their story came to life for me—and for a whole bunch of other people as well. I recently had the honor of meeting Joe and Cheryl in person. The love they have for each other was so obvious you could spot it a mile away—they were carrying on like newlyweds! Her face lit up when she talked about Joe. Tears came to Joe's eyes when he told me in person about how she forgave him. They were the kind of couple that made me want to step outside and call my wife just to tell her how much I love her. And, by the way, I did call her right after my show that night.

These are lyrics from a song I wrote called "Restored" that was inspired by Joe and Cheryl's story:

> *I believe love can be restored*
> *If we take a little less this time*
> *and give a little more*
> *So, hold onto me*
> *I promise you we'll make it through this*
> *stronger than we've ever been before*
> *Let's be the proof that love can be*
> *Restored*[5]

At that concert, I invited Joe and Cheryl up on stage to share their forgiveness story, and I played "Restored." After the concert three married couples came forward for prayer, each in the exact situation Joe and Cheryl had once found themselves in. These couples were on the verge of divorce, but they were so moved by the reconciliation they witnessed in Joe and Cheryl, they began believing that maybe, just maybe, God could restore their marriage as well. That, my friends, is the power of a story.

It's one thing, though, to have a story. It's another thing to tell that story. You better believe Joe was ashamed of his mistakes. Yet the power of forgiveness has set both Joe and Cheryl free to see how God can use what they've been through to help other couples in the same situation. (In fact, Joe's willingness to speak about how he failed as a husband reminds me of Paul proclaiming he was the "worst of sinners" (1 Timothy 1:15 NIV). When God has miraculously healed our broken relationships, we are free from the shame and embarrassment that mistakes can carry with them. We are free to stand up and share our stories with a world that needs to hear. Why? Because just as God used Joe and Cheryl's sharing at the concert, God can use your experience and mine to bring another story out of darkness into the light of a second chance, a light that shines because of forgiveness.

ALICE

It was pitch black and pouring rain as I drove myself and my two boys away from the nightmare we had been living. Afraid of what he would do when he found us missing, I called to tell him we had left. He begged me to stop, to tell him where I was so he could get us. I didn't. I dialed my parents. I drove through the tears and the rain, and my dad kept me driving. He had given me simple instructions: "Drive here and then call me" followed by "Drive here and then call me." Eventually my parents talked me the rest of the way in, while I had only a vague awareness of where we were.

When we arrived at the shelter, the hosts led us to a small room. The boys sat on the floor and played while I answered questions and filled out registration forms. The rules were strict: set curfew; set bedtime; children could not be left unattended; daily chores; no visitors. Then we were shown our room. It had a single bed and a bunk bed. We woke in the morning and went for a walk. With the first step outside the door, I knew we were safe.

The other day I came across the admissions folder for the shelter where we stayed that first night. Inside was the picture that my older son had drawn while waiting for me to register. On that dark, sad, rainy night, he had drawn a picture of a bright sunshiny day. That is how it felt to finally be free from the prison of abuse.

At some point during our ten-year marriage, I conceded and simply accepted the abuse. But with acceptance I was still imprisoned. Now that I have broken free of that prison, I can choose to forgive my former husband's actions, but I no longer choose to accept them. With forgiveness I feel no more anger. Forgiveness allows me greater perspective and helps me see our relationship for what it was.

Forgiveness is, for me, a continuous issue. It is an ongoing process. My abuser is still very much a part of my life because of the boys, so he still has plenty of opportunities to hurt me. Matthew 18:22 (NKJV) comes to mind for me: I will most likely have to forgive him up to seventy times seven times. I know I will struggle in some instances more than others. But if I were not to forgive him, I could not objectively guide my boys through the complications that come with our divorce. Complications that mean they understand on some level why I left their father, but they will also still love him. Forgiveness allows me to tell my boys stories of the good times, memories that show them they come from a place of love.

Most of all I work on forgiving myself. I have long since let go of the idea that I was at fault for the abuse in my marriage. However, I still feel the tremendous weight of the effect this has had on my boys. A mother should protect her children. I failed them. I allowed them to see things no child should ever see. That is not something I can make go away. It happened, and we deal every day with the lasting effects.

FORGIVENESS IS LIKE THE WEATHER

When you hold resentment toward another, you are bound to that person or condition by an emotional link that is stronger than steel. Forgiveness is the only way to dissolve that link and get free.

Catherine Ponder

orgiveness doesn't always mean that reconciliation will follow. In a perfect world, the forgiveness and reconciliation would always go hand in hand. One person says, "I'm sorry," the other person forgives, and then all is right in the world. But Alice's story illustrates that reconciliation is not always an option. She had to endure what no spouse should ever have to experience: verbal, emotional, and even physical abuse at the hands of her husband. For the safety of her young sons, she did a heroic thing, bravely fleeing what she described as a prison even though she knew she would struggle as a single mom trying to make ends meet. The authorities, however, had advised her not to have any contact with her husband because of the dangerous nature of her situation. In circumstances like these, forgiveness is less about mending a relationship and more about healing a painful past so that Alice can finally move on, free from the darkness of years of abuse.

I love how Alice described the morning after that cold, dark, rainy night when she and her boys escaped. Waking up in that shelter and then stepping outside to feel the sunshine that warmed their faces, she and her sons felt free for the first time in a long time. Sure, their journey was just beginning, and Alice knew she and her boys had a long, hard road ahead. But for the first time, they could see the light of hope.

So why, then, is forgiveness still an essential ingredient in Alice's story? Her husband isn't asking for forgiveness. He has shown no signs of remorse for what he put her and the kids through. For the safety of her children, she has to put aside any desire for reconciliation. And, thanks to this man, she must now carry the burden of parenthood on her shoulders alone. For Alice to forgive her abusive husband does not mean that she has to trust him again or ever go back to that dangerous situation. I love how Rick Warren explains the difference between forgiveness and reconciliation or trust: "Forgiveness must be immediate, whether or not a person asks for it. Trust must be rebuilt over time. Trust requires a track record."[6]

But why must forgiveness be immediate? Alice can tell you why. Every morning she wakes up and stares into the eyes of two handsome little boys who I'm sure in some way resemble their father; maybe one has his smile or the other, his laugh. And these boys are watching her. They are looking up to her. These boys need their mom now more than ever. So if Alice spends her days and nights eaten up by anger or buried by bitterness, how can she provide the love and attention the boys need? William

Arthur Ward wrote, "A life lived without forgiveness is a prison."[7] There's that word again, *prison*. This was the same word Alice used to describe the relationship she had escaped. Choosing not to forgive would mean trading one prison for another.

See, forgiveness is like the weather. When it rains, the crops grow. When the crops grow, the farmer's harvest is bountiful. When the harvest is bountiful, people are nourished. But ask a farmer how different the outcome is when there is a drought in the land. When there is no rain, the crops die. When the crops die, the farmer's harvest is destroyed. When the harvest is destroyed, people go hungry. Well, Alice's two young boys are hungry for nourishment. They didn't ask to be born. They were caught in a drought, innocent children finding themselves in a home characterized by violence rather than love. But Alice ended that drought on the night she and her boys drove through the pouring rain to the shelter. And now, as hard as it may be, she must let forgiveness rain over her and her sons. For where there is forgiveness, love grows. And where love grows, people are nourished.

SHARON

My husband and I have served in ministry for over forty years. When we met and fell in love in Bible college many, many years ago, we were just two young people with a burning desire to show God's love to the world. Over the years we've seen the good and the not-so-good parts of church life. At times my faith has been shaken to the point that I wondered where God was in the middle of a given situation. You see, my husband served as senior pastor of a church, and every now and then an individual or a group of individuals would become disgruntled over something they didn't like about the church or about its pastor. Yes, my husband. But instead of going straight to the focus of that grievance, they spread rumors, they gossiped, they stirred up unnecessary conflict, and they attempted to wreak havoc on our ministry. I never expected the sources of my greatest hurt in life to come not from people in the world, but from people inside the walls of a church.

One particular individual in our church was especially hurtful to my husband and our whole family. I prayed and prayed that the issue would be resolved. I prayed that somehow God would protect my children from having their faith negatively affected by the view of church they had from our front-row pew. Finally—and I feel bad for saying *finally*—this person decided to leave the church altogether, but when he did, our church body looked like a small town in the wake of a tornado. I remember praying a prayer of thanksgiving, "Thank You, Lord, that this man no longer has any power over us!" And I felt like the Lord responded to my heart, "He never had any more power over you than you gave him." That was an important lesson that God taught me, and from that point on I began to think about who I was giving the power to.

Through the years, I have had to forgive different Christians who have come and gone, many who did their damage and then left before we could resolve the situation. At the end of the day, the church is not perfect. Those of us in the church are not perfect people. We are all just broken people who need a healing God. And nobody can expect perfection from imperfect people. But at the same time, we in the church need to love one another, not tear one another down. I've seen too much of it in my years of ministry, and I know that Satan knows if he can divide the church, he can weaken its impact on the world. If Satan can get us to judge instead of love, he wins. If he can get us to gossip instead of communicate, he wins. If he can get us to tear one another down instead of build one another up, he wins.

My family and I will continue to serve the Lord. We will continue to try our best to show the love of the Lord to all who walk through the doors of this church. We will not let the evil one win. I just pray that God will keep my heart soft and my children's hearts protected from becoming callous. We will not give power to the evil one. We will love the hurting and trust that, when opposition comes, our God is the One who holds the greater power.

THE PREACHER'S WIFE

Despite a hundred sermons on forgiveness, we do not forgive easily, nor find ourselves easily forgiven. Forgiveness, we discover, is always harder than the sermons make it out to be.

Elizabeth O'Connor[8]

The sign out front might read, "Come as you are," but sadly the people inside the church don't always offer a very warm welcome. Having spent my whole life in and around the church, I can relate to the preacher's wife whose story you just read. I've also seen my fair share of congregations who would prefer you clean up your act before you darken the door of their church.

Philip Yancey knows about this too. He tells of a friend who was working in the inner city of Chicago. When he was talking with a down-and-out prostitute who was ashamed of all the things she had done, Yancey's friend asked the woman if she had ever thought of going to a church for help. This was her response: "Church!" she cried. "Why would I ever go there? I was already feeling terrible about myself. They'd just make me feel worse!"[9] As D. L. Moody observed and that woman experienced, "Of one hundred men, one will read the Bible; the ninety-nine will read the Christian." For that woman to be so adamantly against seeking help from the church, she must have had a wounding experience before, a time when she felt judged by Christians instead of loved.

Perhaps I'm getting ahead of myself, though, by talking about how we Christians need to show love to the world. After all, we can't expect our churches to reach out to a lost and hurting world with love if we in the church can't even love one another the way God calls us to. His command is clear: "Whoever loves God must also love his brother" (1 John 4:21 ESV). Not only are we to love one another, but we are also to encourage one another and keep communication open. "Let us consider how we may spur one another on toward love and good deeds. Let us not give up meeting together, as some are in the habit of doing, but let us encourage one another—and all the more as you see the Day approaching" (Hebrews 10:24–25 NIV).

I like this quote from Harriett Beecher Stowe's *Uncle Tom's Cabin*: "Don't the Bible say we must love everybody? O, the Bible! To be sure, it says a great many things; but, then, nobody ever thinks of doing them."[9] What if that weren't true? What if, when the world looked at us Christians, they saw people united by an undeniable love? Imagine a community where believers truly do "spur one another on." One that communicates in a healthy way when differences arise. One where people are slow to become angry and quick to forgive. I want to be part of a community like that. And I have a feeling the world would too—if that's what they saw when they looked inside a church.

As that preacher's wife has experienced, oftentimes the

opposition we believers encounter doesn't come in the form of angry picketers holding signs. Our opposition comes from fellow believers within our church family. Maybe you've been bruised by another believer. Maybe you've been hurt by someone who professes to be a Christ follower, and you've allowed that disillusioning experience to have a negative impact on your own faith. I understand.

When I was a teenager, I honestly reached a point in my faith where I looked around my church and found myself thinking, *If this is what it looks like to follow God, I'm not sure I want it!* I had been hurt so many times by people whose actions didn't line up with the words we were all singing together on Sunday morning. I will never forget something my dad shared with me during that discouraging time in my journey of faith. He said, "Son, people will let you down. Even God's people will let you down. Your mom and I will let you down. But you must keep your eyes on God at all times. You cannot let your view of God be tainted by the imperfections of His people." That is quite a perspective considering my dad has been a pastor for over forty years.

After that conversation, I knew I needed to forgive some believers who hurt me. Maybe that is true for you as well. After all, in order to show the world the God who loves, we must love one another. To show the world the God who forgives, we must forgive one another.

By the way, the preacher's wife who inspired this chapter? She's my mom. And I can honestly say that I have a personal faith and belief in a forgiving God because of the way I've seen both of my parents walk in humility, forgiving even fellow believers who have hurt them along the way. These two dear people give me hope that our churches everywhere can begin to pull together and really show the world what the warm welcome of love and forgiveness looks like.

I grew up with constant criticism: "You are ugly. You're stupid. You're worthless. You're not good enough for anything. You are useless." You can only hear things like that for so long before you start believing them. I seldom felt loved, and although I wanted love more than anything, I never sought love from boys. All I ever thought was *No one will ever love me. I will never be a mother. I will never amount to anything.*

Through all of that, though, I always felt God near me. He surrounded me in everything I did. He kept me from so many destructive paths, wrong choices, and dangerous situations. I didn't talk to Him, but He never left me. Then, during my senior year of high school, some people where I worked said one of the managers wanted to go out with me. *This must be a trick* was all I could think. But God nudged me to go.

I began dating the man who is now my husband, and I couldn't believe how perfect he was. *How could he like me, let alone love me?* I waited every day for him to break up with me.

After all, what did I have to offer him? Nothing. In fact, we did almost break up once because I told him that I didn't deserve some gifts he'd brought me. He was so hurt, but I couldn't understand why someone—why he—would give me gifts. I had done nothing to deserve them, and I had always been made to believe that I wasn't worthy of a gift.

Thanks to God, my husband didn't leave, and he proposed a year after we started dating. We were married a year and a half later. I was just twenty, and he was twenty-two. Even then, everyone told us we were too young and our marriage would never last. In the back of my mind, I thought that was probably true. *After all,* I used to think, w*hen he truly sees me every day and every night, he will surely move on to someone better.* But he didn't. We have been married for sixteen years and have four wonderful children together.

Even to this day, though, I struggle with thinking I am not good enough in any aspect of my life. Yet God has been good to me and is slowly changing my opinion of myself. But the tape in my mind keeps rewinding automatically and playing over and over again. I wish I could erase it.

A friend of mine leads a prayer and restoration ministry at her church. When I talked with her about this book, she began to tell me how essential she has found forgiveness to be in guiding individuals she prays with toward a place where they can find true healing for their deepest life wounds. Her experiences paralleled what the stories I'd heard had already revealed to me: many people are limping through life, missing out on the chance to experience true joy and happiness, and believing that the burden of unresolved forgiveness issues will never be lifted. Many people feel like Melissa does, wishing they could erase the tape in their mind that replays the hurt over and over again.

What if there *were* a way to erase that tape? Wouldn't you want to learn how? Well, if I didn't believe there is a way to be relieved from the burden of unforgiveness, I wouldn't be writing this book. And if you didn't believe in the value of forgiveness and the freedom that comes with it, you probably wouldn't be reading this book either. What's more, without forgiveness there would never be resolution of any issue. And where there is no resolution, there is no peace.

Consider Billy Graham's simple observation: "Man has two great spiritual needs. One is for forgiveness. The other is for goodness." In reading Melissa's story, you can almost hear her crying out for both forgiveness and goodness. Who doesn't desire those things? My counselor friend shared with me some very practical and biblically sound steps that she leads people through so they can reach the destination of forgiveness and goodness. After all, we can only be reminded of our need to forgive so many times. Without any practical steps to help us get there, we will too easily stay frozen in our unforgiveness.

1. Admit the wrong.

Call the wrong what it is. Talk in detail to someone you trust or write down on a piece of paper the wrong that was done, the wrong that hurt you. Melissa, for instance, described the way her family spoke to her and acknowledged that their constant criticism throughout her childhood was wrong. Lewis B. Smedes describes the importance of this first step: "When we forgive evil we do not excuse it, we do not tolerate it, we do not smother it. We look the evil full in the face, call it what it is, let its horror shock and stun and enrage us, and only then do we forgive it."

2. Admit the hurt.

In what ways did the offense affect you? For example, "That made me feel angry, hurt . . ." Again, in Melissa's story, she was made to feel worthless and unlovable. Acknowledging how a certain behavior or a specific incident hurt you enables you to draw a line between cause and effect, between the offense and the impact it has had on your life.

3. Acknowledge the need.

What Melissa needed from her family was affirmation, not criticism; protection, not rejection. Every little girl needs to be made to feel beautiful, not ugly. You can gain great insight when you think about what you were deprived of when the offending party chose to hurt you instead of help you.

4. Confess any sinful responses.

I trust you are beginning to see the power of this line of thinking. We miss out on the blessings of forgiveness when we don't allow our hearts the time needed to fully process the hurt. It is also important to recognize your negative responses to the hurt. Melissa, for instance, had to confess her conclusion that no one would ever love her. She carried that negative self-image into her marriage, and it threatened the wholeness of her relationship with her husband. The Bible says, "The LORD is my helper, so I will have no fear. What can mere people do to me?" (Hebrews 13:6). It is key to pinpoint what you have allowed other people's actions to do to you. Remember that the Lord is your Helper and that you don't have to let people who have hurt you affect you the way they once did.

5. Release the hurt to Jesus.

Letting go is so much easier said than done. But it is easier to let hurt go when you place it in the hands of the Healer. You can release your hurt to the care of your all-knowing, all-powerful

God who created both you *and* the one who hurt you. He knows the most intimate details of your hurt, and He hurts with you. So pray, "Lord, I release all my hurts and my very self to You. Help me cast all my anxiety on You because You care for me (1 Peter 5:7). Help me accept Your yoke that is easy to bear and the burden You give me that is light (Matthew 11:30)."

6. Bless the one(s) who hurt you.

Many people trip over this step, but to experience the fullness of forgiveness, you cannot afford to skip over it. Hear Jesus' command: "Love your enemies! Pray for those who persecute you!" (Matthew 5:44). When someone has hurt you, the thought of praying for that person will feel counterintuitive, to say the least. But Jesus calls us to pray for our enemies, and when we step out in faith, no matter how hard this step may be, God will honor it. Maybe this prayer will help you get started: "Lord Jesus, if that person has repented, I stand in agreement with that, and I ask that You bless him. If that person has not repented, I ask that You bless her with a relationship with You that leads to repentance and freedom in You."

7. Release the hurt and let the Lord replace it with healing.

"My God will meet all your needs according to his glorious riches in Christ Jesus" (Philippians 4:19 NIV). The Lord knows what each one of us needs. He also knows what we have been deprived of—the love someone withheld when we needed to receive it; the kind words someone left unsaid when we needed to be affirmed. And He will be faithful to fill us up until we thirst no more. If we ask, He will answer us: "Lord Jesus, I ask that You give me what they could not or would not give." Then patiently wait for Jesus to bless you with His healing. Know that, like a shepherd, He will feed His flock, He will carry the lambs in His arms, and hold them close to His heart (Isaiah 40:11).

Your heavenly Father longs for you to walk through this process with Him as He holds you close to His heart. Each step is vital to your healing. We tend to be too quick to jump back up after being knocked to the ground by a deep hurt. Too soon we dust ourselves off and proclaim, "I'm good. I'm fine." That's not living; that's limping. And that is nowhere near as good as life can be if you take the time to place your deepest hurts into the hands of the Healer. The tape can be erased. The message can be replaced. And your deepest wounds can heal. Really heal.

JUSTICE

He has shown you, O mortal, what is good.
And what does the Lord require of you?
To act justly and to love mercy
and to walk humbly with your God.

Micah 6:8 NIV

I n my line of work, travel is a necessity. Last year alone, I performed more than a hundred and ten concerts. I traveled to forty-seven states, some more than once. During one season in the very beginning of my career, I remember playing twenty-one shows in as many days.

It's not uncommon for my band and me to play at a church in Charleston, South Carolina, on a Thursday night and a state fair in Florida on Friday night. What we lose in sleep, we gain in frequent flyer miles! My time in airports gives me a unique window to the world, an always entertaining look at the behavior patterns of travelers I see along the way. After all, I can think of few environments more stressful than an airport. Ever traveled through Chicago's O'Hare International Airport? Or New York's JFK? If you think you can get through one of those places stress-free, well, you can just—as the New Yorkers say—"Fugheddaboutit!" Thousands of people are flying to thousands of destinations. Flights are delayed. Kids are crying. The security checkpoints have you down to your boxers. OK, OK, maybe not that extreme, but you get the point.

From experience, I can tell you that the most stressful time to be at the airport is during the early morning hours. Now, one might think that catching the first flight out of town at sunrise would be the *least* stressful time to spend in an airport. You know, beat the rush. Oh, if only that were true! Instead, you get all the stress that an average day at the airport usually offers plus a hefty dose of grumpy thrown in. Think about it. If you had to wake up at 3:45 a.m. just to get to the airport, just to be told to take your shoes off, just to be told to put your shoes back on, just to wait in line, just to board a plane, just to be handed some free peanuts, you'd probably be a bit grumpy too. I've seen these high-pressure, high-stress situations bring out both the best and the worst in people.

One early morning my band and I prepared to board our flight to the next show. We always purchase early boarding passes so we can be sure that our guitars have room to fly with us. (It is no fun landing in Dubuque, Iowa, with a guitar that's in two pieces.) Well, this particular flight happened to be a full house. We boarded early as usual and found a spot where our guitars could rest safe and sound for the duration of our flight. So we got our guitars settled and then settled in ourselves for a little shut-eye.

Several minutes later a priest boarded the plane. He was dressed in his clerical clothing, white collar and all. He began to search for a space in the overhead compartments to place his carry-on bag when he noticed a guitar case resting precisely where he wanted to put his things. Surprisingly, he began to cause a bit of a commotion. The flight attendant kindly informed him that he would need to hand his bag over to her to check with the rest of the suitcases under the plane. The priest did not like this. The band and I avoided eye contact with one another.

The priest's face began to turn red, looking even brighter against that white collar. Finally, his frustration got the best of him and he blurted out this most ironic response a priest could offer to the situation: "There is no justice in this world!" Then, shooting my guitar player a look of disgust, he handed his bag to the flight attendant and stormed off to find his middle seat on the plane. That was one stressful situation I'm sure the priest would like to do over again if he were given the chance. But in that high-stress moment, he felt he was on the losing end of an unfair situation, and his anger simply got the best of him.

Justice is something that we all feel entitled to. Why wouldn't we feel entitled to a fair shake in life? We all want fairness. That seems reasonable. Except for one thing—and I can still hear the voice of my sixth-grade teacher. After I told her that my dog ate my homework and it wasn't *fair* that she wouldn't grant me an extra day to turn it in, she said, "Life isn't fair." And she was right. In many ways, our life and especially our character will develop according to how we handle injustice, those moments when we are treated unfairly, those times when the world takes what you believe to be rightfully yours.

Nelson Mandela was forced to spend twenty-seven years of his life in prison. Why? Because he directed peaceful, nonviolent protests against the South African government and its racist policies. Since Mandela was clearly a victim of the great injustice of apartheid, one might expect him to come out of prison swinging, ready to fight for revenge. Instead, he continued in his peaceful push for progress and, at age seventy-seven, was elected South Africa's first black president. From there he continued to work to unify South Africans by encouraging reconciliation and forgiveness.

The movie *Invictus* is set in the 1990s during Mandela's time as president and as the Rugby World Cup was being played. He saw sports as a way of bringing the country together. In one gripping scene, he encourages the national sports federation, whose members were predominantly black, to support the Springboks, a predominantly white South African national team. In the film, Mandela says, "Our enemy is no longer the Afrikaner. . . . We have to surprise them with compassion, with restraint, and generosity. I know all of the things they denied us. But this is no time to celebrate petty revenge." In another scene, Francois Pienaar, the white captain of the Springboks team, was wondering aloud to his wife about Mandela: "I was thinking of how you spend thirty years in a tiny cell and come out ready to forgive the people who put you there." Mandela himself answered that question in this statement: "As I walked out the door toward the gate that would lead to my freedom, I knew if I didn't leave my bitterness and hatred behind, I'd still be in prison."

Jesus provided us with clear instructions for how to handle injustice: "If someone slaps you on one cheek, offer the other cheek also. If someone demands your coat, offer your shirt also" (Luke 6:29). But Jesus didn't stop at merely *telling* us what to do: He *showed* us how to do it. His last days were riddled with one injustice after the other. Did He fight back? No. When an angry crowd arrived with Judas to arrest Jesus, His disciples asked, "Lord, should we fight? We brought the swords!" Scripture says, "One of them struck at the high priest's slave, slashing off his right ear." What did Jesus do? "Jesus said, 'No more of this.' And he touched the man's ear and healed him" (Luke 22:49–51). Later, during Jesus' trial, as the false accusations about Him were flying around, the high priest asked Him, "Well, aren't you going to answer these charges? What do you have to say for yourself?" Scripture says, "Jesus remained silent" (Matthew 26:62–63).

We are called not to fight for justice, but to show restraint in the face of injustice. We are not to lash out with angry words in our defense; we are to respond peacefully or even remain silent, as Jesus did. Philip Yancey wrote, "By forgiving another, I am trusting that God is a better justice-maker than I am. . . . I leave in God's hands the scales that must balance justice and mercy."[10] If we want the world to see Jesus, then no matter how unfairly we are treated, no matter what injustice is done, we must keep Jesus' example front and center in our heart and mind every single day. We must put away our sword and ask God for the strength to follow Jesus' example and surprise the world with compassion.

Forgiveness

It's the opposite of how you feel
When the pain they caused is just too real
Takes everything you have to say the word

Forgiveness

KRYSTAL

My father is an alcoholic. My mother was the caregiver and repeatedly chose him over us kids. I spent all my time and energy protecting. I sustained all forms of abuse because no one was ever there to protect *me*. I had to protect my sisters and myself. It reached the point where I needed to know what type of alcohol my father was drinking on a given night because different alcohols made him act out in different ways. I had to learn this to know if this was a night that I should lock my sisters and myself in the bathroom, pretend we were sleeping, or leave the house altogether until morning.

Living like this, I felt like even God had rejected me. I have always wondered, *Where were You, God? How could You let me suffer like this? How could You let my sisters suffer? Why didn't You help? Didn't You care? Don't You care?* Yet inside there was a tiny spark of hope that God really did care about what was happening to me, that He really did love me.

As I got older, I convinced myself that my life was normal. I minimized so many of my feelings just to survive. And I survived only as a victim. But never once did I forget God. I wanted to believe that He had always been there even when I was in dangerous situations.

God began working in me years ago through a dream. This dream has shaped and molded my life. In this dream, I always saw myself running toward a little five-year-old girl who was holding a teddy bear. All over her body were these things that looked like leaches. They were trying to hurt her, and I was trying to reach her before they did. But I never got there in time. I'd see the little girl start to cry, and then I would wake up.

I spent six months at a wonderful place called Mercy Ministries, a home that works to restore the lives of girls struggling like me. God really met me there, and I began to deal with the trauma of my past once and for all. At Mercy we tackled ten years of healing in six months. I had to learn how to trust people again. I also had to learn to trust God because I had sometimes felt like He abandoned me. One of the biggest things God showed me during my recovery was this: *Sometimes what we think of as rejection is really protection.* I can understand and see it now: God didn't abandon me while I was being abused. He was with me then, and He is with me now. He has protected me all this time—and all that I have experienced is for His glory.

I know you don't know me, but I am a walking testimony to God's power and love. I would certainly be dead if it weren't for God and for Mercy intervening the way they did. Now, because I know the love of Christ, I am able to hold my head up high. I am a daughter of the King. And I have realized that the little girl I was always trying to save in my dream was . . . me. I know I can't go back and avoid all that pain—but I don't have to because God's love and His grace are amazing. This joy I have for the first time in my life makes me cry. For the first time I feel alive. I am twenty-seven years old, and I now know peace.

God can and does heal the broken. And He can use my story to help other girls who have been broken like me.

WHERE WERE YOU, GOD?

She wept for innocence lost. She wept for wounds that had never healed. She wept because she blamed herself. And she wept as she asked a question that many have asked from the depths of immeasurable pain. It's the cry of a shattered heart: "Where were You, God?"

The dream that Krystal had again and again for all those

years painted a vividly haunting picture of how she felt inside for so long: utterly abandoned. Abandoned by her alcoholic father. Abandoned by her mother who enabled. Abandoned by everyone who should have protected her. Abandoned by God. Parents are supposed to love their children. To provide for any needs. To nurture, not neglect. Sadly, Krystal missed out on all that because her father and mother were too broken themselves to be what she needed them to be for her, and as a result Krystal's life spun out of control.

Yet before Krystal could ever reach a point where she was able to forgive her father and mother, she needed to address her most immediate need: finding peace with God. She was angry at God and confused about why He had allowed this abuse to happen. When we are wronged by someone whom we should be able to trust, especially in such negligent and abusive ways as Krystal's story depicted, our anger at God and what we felt was His absence takes center stage. We need to deal with this main issue before we can ever even begin the process of forgiving those who actually wronged us.

So where *was* God? Where was God when Krystal and her sisters were hiding in the bathroom? Where was God all those nights when Krystal cried herself to sleep? Where was God when she was desperately praying that her dad would pass out from drunkenness before he visited her bedroom? Was God simply not paying attention? Did He have better things to do?

Years ago my father went to visit with a neighbor who had just lost his daughter to leukemia and, on the same day, found out his mother had been brutally attacked in a home invasion. As a minister for almost forty years, my father has spent many tear-filled nights offering support and comfort to grieving individuals and families during times of tragedy. As my father entered the family's home, the heartbroken man whose life had collapsed in a matter of hours saw him and with a burst of anger he shouted, "Where is your God now, Reverend? Where is your God now?"

My dad returned home late that night and was visibly shaken by the experience. I asked him, "Dad, what did you say to him when he asked you where God was?"

"Nothing," my dad said. "I was wondering the same thing myself."

Even my dad—a man of God like few I've ever met, a man who knows the Bible like the back of his hand, who has read and studied and preached of God's faithfulness—struggled to see how God could possibly be at work in this unthinkable tragedy.

"Jesus wept" (John 11:35 NIV). Known as the shortest verse

in the Bible, these two words appear in the middle of the story of Lazarus, the brother of Mary and Martha and a friend of Jesus. When Lazarus got sick, his sisters, knowing that Jesus was able to do great miracles, sent a message to Him: "Lord, the one you love is sick" (John 11:3 NIV). The sisters were hoping that Jesus would head straight to Lazarus and make him well. Jesus' response? He responded with words rather than action: "This sickness will not end in death. No, it is for God's glory so that God's Son may be glorified through it" (v. 4). Then, instead of rushing to heal Lazarus, Jesus "stayed where he was two more days" (v. 6).

Well, by the time Jesus arrived, Lazarus had already been in the tomb for four days. Four days! So much for fashionably late! When Mary and Martha saw Him, they each took turns basically asking, "Where were You?" "When Mary reached the place where Jesus was . . . she fell at His feet and said, 'Lord, if you had been here, my brother would not have died'" (v. 32). The sisters' questions revealed their disappointment, but Jesus' response revealed much more:

> When Jesus saw her weeping . . . he was deeply moved in spirit and troubled. "Where have you laid him?" he asked.

"Come and see, Lord," they replied.

Jesus wept. (John 11:33–35 NIV)

Jesus grieved with Martha and Mary. He had come to be with them, to share in their pain. He could have healed Lazarus from a distance. He could have stayed where He was even longer than two days. But Jesus went to be with those who were grieving, He wept with them, and *then* He raised Lazarus from the dead. It was more than Jesus' power on display that day. Those people who had gathered at Lazarus's tomb witnessed His compassionate presence as well.

When we ask the question, "Where were You, God?" we are essentially blaming Him for what we see as something that could have been prevented had He intervened. We are saying, "This pain could have been avoided, but You didn't stop it. Why?" Mary and Martha were convinced that if Jesus had arrived a little sooner, Lazarus would still be alive. But after the stone was rolled away and their brother was brought back to life, the sisters' blaming gave way to blessing. Their trust was restored by the One who shared their tears.

Like Martha and Mary in the wake of Lazarus's death, Krystal blamed God for abandoning her during all those years of her abusive childhood. But once Krystal realized that God had brought her to a place of healing, she began to see purpose in her troubled past: she now has a passionate desire to reach out to other girls who have been broken by similar situations. Through both of these stories, we can see that God answers our questions and responds to our blame with His presence, His power, and His purpose: "It is for God's glory so that God's Son may be glorified through it" (John 11:4 NIV).

May you be encouraged today by this simple but profound truth: your hurt hurts the heart of God. We live in a broken world where the combination of sin and the free will to choose sin leaves many people wandering through the wreckage of a painful past and wondering where God was. He *was* with you, and He *is* with you. "The LORD is close to the brokenhearted and saves those who are crushed in spirit" (Psalm 34:18 NIV).

God can handle our questions. He already knows our hearts, so our questions, our doubts, our blame do not surprise Him. Krystal had to learn how to trust God again. Maybe you do too. Maybe you've been blaming God for a painful part of your life, and it's time to forgive Him. I know it is weird to think about forgiving God. But just as God can handle your questions, He can also handle your need to forgive Him so you can begin to learn to trust Him again. And as you begin to place your trust in God completely, He will lead you toward the next step, that of forgiving those who have wronged you.

Krystal asked God over and over again where He was during her abuse. Today she knows that she was never actually alone. Jesus promised His people, "I am with you always, to the very end of the age" (Matthew 28:20 NIV). She no longer needs to dream that painful dream where she tried to protect herself as a little girl. Jesus was weeping with her just as He did with Mary and Martha. Jesus did not abandon Krystal. So when we ask God where He was during our tragedies, our abuse, our trials, He will answer us. This is another of God's promises: "Call to Me, and I will answer you, and show you great and mighty things, which you do not know" (Jeremiah 33:3 NKJV). God will answer us the way He answered Mary, Martha, and Krystal: with His power, His presence, and His purpose. As He does, our blame will subside, our trust in Him will be renewed, and we can begin the process of forgiving others.

I was given up for adoption when I was born. For the last eighteen years, I have searched for my birth parents. I had always wondered if I had my father's eyes or maybe my mom's hair. I wanted to find them. I wanted to know why they didn't want me. I wanted them to tell me why they gave me away. Finally, after all those years of searching, I found my birth father. He agreed to see me, so we made arrangements to meet for the first time ever.

I will never forget that day. I was so scared, but excited at the same time. I'd never had a chance to be his little girl. I hoped that maybe this could be the start of a relationship I had longed for my whole life. I looked my father in the eyes for the first time, and the first thing he said to me was, "You were just a mistake." I have carried those words with me ever since, and I've had the hardest time moving on from that hurtful moment. I don't know if I can ever forgive him for giving me up—or for those hurtful words that broke my heart all over again.

Reading this story hurt my heart. I don't even know this young woman, but I found myself feeling so angered by the thought that anyone would ever have to hear such damaging words. "You were just a mistake" was salt in the already deep wound of abandonment that she carried from knowing that her parents gave her up at birth. First "unwanted"; now "a mistake." How can someone who's been abandoned even begin the process of forgiveness when the hurt is so profound? Perhaps we can learn a few lessons from the story of Joseph.

Like Anonymous, Joseph was unwanted. His father, Jacob, loved Joseph. In fact, Scripture says, "Jacob loved Joseph more than any of his other children because Joseph had been born to him in his old age" (Genesis 37:3). Jacob gave Joseph a beautiful robe, a coat of many colors. As one might imagine, Joseph's brothers were not cool with this. Joseph may have been Jacob's favorite son, but he quickly became his brothers' least favorite sibling: "his brothers hated Joseph because their father loved him more than the rest of them. They couldn't say a kind word to him" (v. 4). To make matters worse, Joseph had some dreams that led him to believe that someday he would rule over all the land, including his father and his brothers. As one might imagine, this interpretation did not improve his standing with his brothers. So the brothers made a plot to kill Joseph, but then wound up going easy on him and instead decided to sell him off as a slave. That's brotherly love for you.

The Bible says, "The LORD was with Joseph, so he succeeded in everything he did as he served in the home of his Egyptian master" (Genesis 39:2). After several years, Joseph's dreams became reality as he rose from the status of a slave to a position of great power. Pharaoh made Joseph second-in-command, and all the people had to submit to him, including his brothers who were now in great need because of a famine in their land. The tables had indeed turned, and now Joseph found himself in a position to repay his brothers for the hurt and the separation they had caused.

If you read Joseph's entire story, he was clearly conflicted about whether to forgive his brothers or get revenge. His choice to forgive did not come overnight. He labored over his decision between justice and mercy. Joseph "broke down and wept. He wept so loudly the Egyptians could hear him" (Genesis 45:2). Even for this hero of the faith, forgiveness did not come easily—and it's easy to understand why. His brothers had literally thrown him away. His own flesh and blood were the reason he spent all those years in slavery.

But now, years later, Joseph had a different perspective on that series of events. He was seeing things from a much broader vantage point. He could see that God had orchestrated even their evil actions to lead him to this great position of power and eventually fulfill those prophecies revealed in dreams years before. God transformed his brothers' curse into Joseph's blessing. And this priceless perspective ultimately led Joseph to experience the freedom of forgiveness when he revealed his identity to his brothers: "I am Joseph, your brother, whom you sold into slavery in Egypt. But don't be upset, and don't be angry with yourselves for selling me to this place. It was God who sent me here ahead of you to preserve your lives" (Genesis 45:4–5).

As Scripture says, "The LORD was with Joseph" (Genesis 39:2). And so once again Joseph succeeded. He succeeded where many of us have failed. Joseph took a leap toward forgiveness, a choice that enabled his relationship with his family to start over again. Joseph not only forgave his brothers for what they had done, but he didn't even blame them—and he told them not to be angry with themselves. Then Joseph promised to take care of his entire family so they would be protected from the famine. Lewis B. Smedes wrote, "You will know that forgiveness has begun when you recall those who hurt you and feel the power to wish them well."[12] Joseph had reached that point where he was willing not only to forgive his brothers but also to look after their well-being. How was this transformation possible for Joseph? Because he understood that God's plan was bigger than his brothers' plan. Joseph told them, "You intended to harm me, but God intended it all for good" (Genesis 50:20).

One more thing, especially if you've ever felt like our anonymous friend. God's promises prove that you are not a mistake. He says, "I know the plans I have for you . . . plans to prosper you and not to harm you, plans to give you hope and a future" (Jeremiah 29:11 NIV). God's bold assertion that He has a plan and a purpose for your life is enough evidence for every single one of us—the abandoned, the unwanted, the discarded, the rejected—to believe that we are here on this earth for a reason. Maybe you've yet to reach the point that Joseph reached, blessed with a perspective that can look back and see why you had to endure hardship at the hands of someone who made you feel unwanted. Maybe the wounds are still fresh, and you are believing the lies that abandonment whispers. Cling tight, then, to the promise that God has good plans for you. Just as He led Joseph out of slavery, He will lead you. He will lead you to a place where you will discover the power of perspective, and the freedom of forgiveness just like Joseph did. Ask God, "Why?" and He will answer you. In His time, He will show you. And His time might not be on this side of heaven. But just as He enabled Joseph, God will give you the strength and the perspective to look those who abandoned you in the eyes and proclaim, "You intended to harm me, but God intended it for good!"

ASKING FOR FORGIVENESS

Forgiveness

It flies in the face of all your pride
Moves away the mad inside
It's always anger's own worst enemy

Even when the jury and the judge
Say you've got to hold a grudge
It's the whisper in the your ear saying, "Set it free"

Forgiveness

LINDA

One of my daughters and I haven't spoken in years. She's married now and has children of her own. My grandchildren don't even know who I am. For a long time I refused to believe that any blame for this situation could fall on me. But if I'm being honest, I know that isn't true. My whole life has always revolved around me. My drinking. My drug use. My boyfriends. All of this while my daughters were left to fend for themselves. I never really knew how to be a mom to them. I moved where I wanted to move even though it meant they had to be uprooted from one school after another. At best, I was more of a friend at times. At worst, I was a neglectful parent who subjected them to things no child should have to experience. My pride has kept me from admitting this to my estranged daughter directly. Instead, I've chosen to live only minutes away from her happy family, claiming that they are the reason for the separation. I have reached out to her only when I needed money, and now I fear that the bridge between us has been completely burned. Now it just feels like too much time has passed for this relationship to be fixed. Even if I did apologize, I'm scared that she would not trust my intentions because of all the times I have asked for money. It's just a horrible mess. Years ago, I guess I just thought everything would work itself out over time. I was wrong, and now I'm afraid there's nothing that can be done.

TIME HEALS NO WOUNDS

I'm convinced that whoever coined the phrase, "Time heals all wounds," was really just afraid of dealing with conflict. The reality is that as time passes, cracks can become canyons, harsh words spark all-out wars, and the slightest leak can make a levee break. Just ask the Hatfields and the McCoys, the Beatles and Yoko Ono, Tom and Jerry. OK, I know that last one is just a cartoon, but like their little cat-and-mouse game, we can go around and around in our relationships and, over time, friends can turn into fierce enemies. History's famous feuds are proof that this saying may sound real nice, but it could not be further from the truth.

I came across one such example that happened to be dripping with irony as well as ice cream. In 1935 the Blake brothers opened their first ice cream shop that would eventually grow into the popular East Coast chain known as Friendly's. These Massachusetts siblings had no idea how difficult it can be for family to be in business together, especially when large amounts of money are involved. Over the years, the Blakes experienced great success, expanding the chain and ultimately selling to the Hershey Foods Corporation, and then being sold again. Until 2007, both brothers appeared to be in friendly agreement as to how the sales of the company were being conducted. But then, as the company faced another possible sale, the younger brother, Curtis, resisted his older brother's intentions, and their relationship became not so friendly. Curtis wrote his older brother, Prestley, a letter pleading with him not to allow the sale of the company. His brother responded publicly via *The Boston Globe*: "I'm sorry my brother isn't with me on this, but I'm going to keep going because I know I'm right." This disagreement simultaneously began the brothers' business feud and ended their friendship. In the same *Boston Globe* piece, Curtis wrote, "I'm very disappointed. [Prestley] was my best friend for 85 years. It would have been a nice story if we ended up best friends for our entire life."[1]

Notice the finality with which he spoke of the feud with his older brother: "It would have been a nice story . . ." He clearly deemed their relationship beyond repair. It was not as though one brother passed away before the two had a chance to resolve their differences. They were both still living, and I'm sure both had working phones. They could have attempted to make amends, but too much time had passed for them to see that as a realistic possibility. These powerful and wealthy businessmen lacked the power to resolve conflict in one of the closest relationships any man can have with another—that of a brother.

Martin Luther King Jr. wrote, "We must develop and maintain the capacity to forgive. He who is devoid of the power to forgive is devoid of the power to love. . . . There is some good in the worst of us and some evil in the best of us. When we discover this, we are less prone to hate our enemies."[2] To decide that a relationship is past the point of no return is to turn a blind eye to the truth of what Dr. King was explaining, that there is "some good in the worst of us and some evil in the best of us." Often it is our inability or our unwillingness to examine our own role in a conflict that allows the clock to keep ticking until too much time has passed. John F. Kennedy's mother, Rose

Kennedy, wrote, "It has been said, 'Time heals all wounds.' I do not agree. The wounds remain. In time, the mind, protecting its sanity, covers them with scar tissue and the pain lessens. But it is never gone."[3]

No, time will not heal all wounds. And we do not possess enough power within to heal them ourselves. Only Jesus can heal our brokenness and our broken relationships: "He heals the brokenhearted and binds up their wounds" (Psalm 147:3 NIV). And no matter how much time has passed, God promises that He is the One "who is able, through his mighty power at work within us, to accomplish infinitely more than we might ask or think" (Ephesians 3:20). You might be staring at a severed relationship, hopeless and thinking that reconciliation is impossible at this point. But Jesus said, "Humanly speaking, it is impossible. But with God everything is possible" (Matthew 19:26).

These verses are not just fluffy promises we can throw around and then sit back to see whether or not God comes through. These verses are foundations of wisdom and truth upon which we can begin rebuilding what has been broken or even destroyed. God calls us to be proactive about conflict resolution, and when we are, we may witness the "impossible."

- "Come to terms quickly with your accuser." (Matthew 5:25 ESV)
- "The beginning of strife is like letting out water, so quit before the quarrel breaks out." (Proverbs 17:14 ESV)
- "Never pay back evil with more evil. Do things in such a way that everyone can see you are honorable. Do all that you can to live in peace with everyone." (Romans 12:17–18)

For Linda, these truths mean picking up the phone or putting pen to paper and taking the first step in confessing her responsibility in the situation. Linda has to humble herself and ask God to give her the courage to take that first step and the faith to believe that He can and will do the impossible, that He can and will restore her relationship with her daughters. Linda must take the first step in building the bridge that she herself burned, but she does not have to do it alone. Neither do you.

- "I will go before you . . . and level the mountains." (Isaiah 45:2)
- "See, I am doing a new thing! Now it springs up; do you not perceive it? I am making a way in the desert and streams in the wasteland." (Isaiah 43:19 NIV)

Some of the greatest modern-day miracles are ones that happen under the radar: these miracles are the miraculous healing of once-ravaged relationships. Placed in the hands of our Healer, the impossible becomes possible. Kids can finally know their grandmother. Mothers and daughters can embrace for the first time in years. Holidays can become anticipated events, not dreaded days. The rough places can be made smooth. But time is ticking. Chances are a relationship in your life needs some extra attention. Don't let another second pass by without making every effort to live in peace with others. Don't wait for time to heal your wounds; ask your Savior to.

GEORGE

My brother and I used to be really close. Even as adults, we both got married, had kids, and lived just a couple towns away from each other. We went to the same church, spent Christmas Eve together exchanging gifts, and had some great times together. We were close. Not anymore.

I can't even remember what it was that got me upset, but I let it drive a wedge between my brother and me and between our families. The relationship never recovered. We went from having a weekly supper together after church on Sundays to going years without seeing each other. He reached out to me, but I was too angry. I wouldn't let go of it, and I wish I had. For many years regret has weighed on me.

I recently began reaching out to my brother, and we have slowly begun to rebuild our friendship. But our kids are grown, and I think about all that we missed out on, how we could have shared in each other's lives all those years. It's crazy how, decades later, I can't even remember what set off our feud in the first place. I guess that just proves how foolish it was to let that event ruin a relationship, especially one with my own brother. I'm not proud of this part of my story, but I've learned from it—and I hope someone else will too.

 ## SIDE EFFECTS

Have you noticed the increasing number of commercials for prescription medications? These commercials crack me up! On any given day you turn on the TV you are bound to view one of these brilliantly produced mini movies that is sure to make you want to run out the door and straight to your doctor for a prescription. The other day I saw an advertisement for a new medication to help treat depression. Allow me to set the scene . . .

It's a beautiful, spring day, and the flowers are in bloom. A puppy is running through a meadow, or maybe a couple in love is riding a bicycle built for two down an old country road. And the music? Well, the music strikes a perfect balance between urgency (so that you remember you need help) and hope (so that you have confidence that this pill will do the trick). It's the soundtrack of the wonderful life that's waiting for you. While all of this is going on, a narrator begins to speak in (of course) the most pleasant voice possible about this new medication that is sure to cure what ails you.

But at this point the commercial takes a subtle turn for the worse, and you may not even realize it. After spending fifteen seconds talking about how this new medication will most assuredly make your life better, the narrator—still speaking in the most pleasant of voices—begins to read a list of possible side effects that may occur while taking this medication. And for the next forty-five seconds (which feels like an eternity) this is what you hear: "A list of possible side effects from taking Axi-ro-mor-onic [I made up that name; it's not a real prescription] may include: difficulty sleeping, difficulty waking up, uncontrollable vomiting, loss of hearing, temporary paralysis, unwanted facial hair, bad breath, spontaneous nosebleeds, a tingling sensation in your abdomen, allergic reaction to babies, loss or shortness of breath, lack of bladder control, sudden urges to rob a bank, difficulty remembering your own name, a strange craving for prune juice, chronic athlete's foot, and a fear of large bodies of water." And just when you think the narrator has finished reading the list of side effects, the voice begins again: "Other possible side effects include allergic reactions to cotton, possible heart attack, body rash, violent temper toward people who wear purple . . ." You get the idea.

And do you know what images are flashing across the screen while this less than appealing list of horrible side effects is listed? You guessed it. That cute puppy is still running freely through the field. That lovely couple is even happier, having stopped for a picnic in that field of wildflowers. Matter of fact, if you had the volume down on your television and could only watch the commercial without hearing it, you'd think the medication had absolutely no side effects at all. But when you turn up the volume, even all the positive spin in the world cannot hide the reality that while this pill may help treat one symptom, there's also a good chance there will be side effects.

How would life be different if the choices you and I have to make came with a list of side effects like those commercials offer? "Warning! Possible side effects of cheating on your spouse include eternal regret, heartbroken children, trust that will be almost impossible to rebuild, and an incredible amount of shame." All the fluffy puppies in the world wouldn't be able to cover up those side effects! I can't help but think that being reminded of the consequences of our actions would most definitely affect our choices. There are, without a doubt, side effects to many of the choices we make in life. The same is true when we choose forgiveness—and unforgiveness.

A surprising number of studies have explored how forgiveness—or the lack thereof—affects the human body. Harvard researchers found that mentally nursing a grudge puts your body through the same strain as a significantly stressful event: muscles tense, blood pressure rises, and sweating increases. Over time, this chronic stress plus the flood of stress hormones such as adrenaline and cortisol can have a dramatically negative impact on the immune system. Research aside, I like how Anne Lamott describes the side effects: "Not forgiving is like drinking rat poison and then waiting for the rat to die."[4]

Like those TV ads, the Bible warns us of the negative side effects of unforgiveness. These include:

- **Disorder**: "If you harbor bitter envy and selfish ambition in your hearts . . . there you find disorder and every evil practice." (James 3:14, 16 NIV)
- **More Unforgiveness**: "If you forgive men their trespasses, your heavenly Father will also forgive you. But if you do not forgive men their trespasses, neither

will your Father forgive your trespasses." (Matthew 6:14–15 NKJV)

- **Lies**: "If someone says, 'I love God,' and hates his brother, he is a liar; for he who does not love his brother whom he has seen cannot love God whom he has not seen." (1 John 4:20 ESV)
- **Blindness**: "Whoever lacks these qualities is so nearsighted that he is blind, having forgotten that he was cleansed from his former sins." (2 Peter 1:9 ESV)

God desires for us to pay attention to these side effects and live accordingly. "Dear friends, let us love one another, for love comes from God" (1 John 4:7 NIV).

On the flip side, if we love one another and forgive one another the way God commands us to, we will experience the positive side effects that He has promised. Some side effects will most definitely include:

- **Reward**: "If your enemy is hungry, give him food to eat; if he is thirsty, give him water to drink . . . The LORD will reward you." (Proverbs 25:21–22 NIV)
- **Knowing God**: "Dear friends, let us love one another, for

love comes from God. Everyone who loves has been born of God and knows God." (1 John 4:7 NIV)

- **Holiness**: "Make every effort to live in peace with everyone and to be holy." (Hebrews 12:14 NIV)

Other wonderful side effects will include "love, joy, peace, patience, kindness, goodness, faithfulness, gentleness, and self-control" (Galatians 5:22–23).

As stated before, God desires for us to pay attention to these side effects and to live accordingly. But Satan comes to "steal and kill and destroy" our relationships and our lives (John 10:10). Like those prescription drug commercials, the Enemy will do his best to mask the side effects of unforgiveness. But one thing I noticed at the end of the commercials is that the narrator always says, "Ask your doctor if this medicine is right for you." When it comes to forgiveness, all we have to do is ask our Savior which choice is right for us. If we let Him, He will guide us and empower us to walk the path that leads to restoration, reconciliation, and peace with others. These side effects will most definitely improve the quality of your life.

DAVID

My story is like that of many fathers whose children lose their way.

God blessed my wife and me with two beautiful daughters. Every day we did our best to equip them to walk the walk of faith. Every day we would send our children out the door with "Remember whose child you are!" They would smile with childlike faith and point to heaven. The years passed so quickly, and too soon my eldest, Jessica, was no longer a little girl, but a woman. The day came when she gave her heart to a man who led her away from her faith and family and down a dark road of abuse. Whenever I reached out to her, she would tell me, "I'm not that same little girl anymore, Daddy."

A thousand sleepless nights, tear-stained pillows, hours battling on our knees—my wife and I felt so helpless. It is in those dark times of life we have to tell ourselves to be faithful, to be strong, to never give up, God is faithful, endure! But I didn't want to endure. I wanted to hold my little girl safe in my arms as I did when she was a child. Yet the storm raged on. God does not promise that He will calm all our storms. What He does promise is to hold on to us through them. I can tell you now, He is faithful!

Late one night the call came: "Mommy and Daddy, can I come home?" We greeted Jessica at the door with open arms. Trembling, shattered by the world, torn by abuse, she was home. In the days that followed, she told me, "Daddy, I never forgot whose child I was. Jesus held me through it all. It was a long journey home, but I will be all right." Today Jessica is healing in the arms of her father and her heavenly Father. By her side now is her six-year-old "little man of faith" whom I was privileged to baptize. He is our family legacy.

We are so torn, tattered, and broken by this world. Sometimes I just want to call my heavenly Father and say, "Daddy, can I come home?" I know He will be there to embrace me just as I embraced my own daughter. But until then I will point my finger toward heaven and say, "Father, let me not forget whose child I am."

I will always remember the day our daughter walked back through the door of our home. When our eyes met and we embraced, she didn't have to ask for forgiveness. It was already hers! My love for her wouldn't allow me to keep score of failures, sins, or broken promises. She is my child.

It is to the prodigals . . . that the memory of their father's
house comes back. If the son had lived economically, he
would never have thought of returning.

Simone Weil

One of the strongest opponents of forgiveness is fear. "What if I say I'm sorry and the person doesn't accept my apology?" "Have I run out of second chances with this person?" "What if that person doesn't want to forgive me?" I have a good feeling these are some of the questions that kept David's daughter, Jessica, away from home for so long. After all, she had turned her back on the ones who loved her most. All of her plans had failed. She was struggling with the shame of knowing how deeply she had hurt her family and was afraid that the door she had slammed shut when she walked out was a door that could never again be opened. But the Bible holds a powerful promise that speaks directly to our fear of rejection: "There is no fear in love. But perfect love drives out fear" (1 John 4:18 NIV).

And so, when a young woman reached the end of her rope

and her steps had taken her to the end of that wayward road, her memory of her father's love for her flooded her thirsty heart. She recalled his words: "Remember whose child you are." Jessica longed to be that little girl once again. She began to believe that maybe—just maybe—those shadows of fear could be banished by the reminder of how much she was loved and the hope that she might still be loved. And what did Jessica find when she returned home? Her parents welcomed her with open arms and much rejoicing, prompting her to wonder, I'm sure, why she had waited so long to go home.

These are lyrics to a song I wrote called "Love Stands Waiting" that were inspired by David's story about Jessica:

> *Whoever said you can't go back?*
> *Whoever sold you a lie like that?*
> *Whoever said you could fall too far?*
> *Did you forget who's child you are?*
>
> *Truth is, I've been counting the days*
> *Till my tear-filled eyes see your beautiful face*
> *and I leave every light on to lead you home*
> *So come home, come home, come home*

Love stands waiting for your return
Love stands hoping you'll come back from
Wherever you were
And when you can't stand on your own anymore
Love stands waiting
So what are you waiting for?[5]

Jesus surely knew that fear would forever serve as a fierce deterrent to our asking for and receiving forgiveness. He understood that fear would try to keep our hearts from returning home to the warm embrace of forgiveness. I wonder if that is one reason Jesus painted three powerful pictures of pursuit and forgiveness, back to back to back, in Luke 15. There He told the story of the lost sheep, the lost coin, and, finally, the lost son, and His third parable is almost a mirror image of the story David wrote to me about his daughter. A son went to his father, asked for his inheritance, left home, and "squandered his wealth in wild living" (Luke 15:13 NIV). At his lowest point, the son hired himself out as a servant, feeding the pigs, and Scripture says, "He longed to fill his stomach with the pods that the pigs were eating" (Luke 15:16 NIV).

Question: Do you think the son's change in fortune happened

overnight? I have a feeling he knew he was beginning to run out of money long before he found himself hanging with the pigs. So why didn't he return home earlier? A strong contender for that answer could be fear—the fear of facing the people he had hurt, fear that they would reject him. But read what happened when this young man "came to his senses" (Luke 15:17 NIV):

> "He got up and went to his father.
>
> "But while he was still a long way off, his father saw him and was filled with compassion for him; he ran to his son, threw his arms around him and kissed him.
>
> "The son said to him, 'Father, I have sinned against heaven and against you. I am no longer worthy to be called your son.'
>
> "But the father said to his servants, 'Quick! Bring the best robe and put it on him. Put a ring on his finger and sandals on his feet. Bring the fattened calf and kill it. Let's have a feast and celebrate. For this son of mine was dead and is alive again; he was lost and is found.' So they began to celebrate." (Luke 15:20–24 NIV)

One of the things I love most about this passage is how the son began by attempting to apologize to his father, but his father didn't even acknowledge what he heard. He was too busy beginning the celebration! "Quick! Bring the best robe and put it on him . . . Let's have a feast and celebrate. For this son of mine was dead and is alive again!" Can you imagine what the son felt when he heard those words? Jessica knows how the prodigal son felt. You can too.

Is fear keeping you from returning home today—home to your family, home to your spouse, home to your Savior? Remember this: there is no fear in love. "Perfect love drives out fear" (1 John 4:18 NIV). Forgiveness is never easy, it's rarely simple, and it's often messy. David and his daughter can tell you that they didn't become a completely whole family overnight. They had much to work through in the days, weeks, and months that followed Jessica's return as God restored what once was a broken family. But taking the first step away from fear and toward forgiveness is what allowed the healing to begin.

Is there a broken relationship in your life that needs healing? If so, let David and Jessica's inspiring story remind you today that God's perfect love for you can cast out fear. Remember whose child you are. Go home. And let the celebration begin!

DON'T LET THE SUN GO DOWN

I came across the true story of a couple in Cambodia who separated after forty years of marriage. Unfortunately, that in itself is not shocking news. I'm sure all of us have heard the statistics: approximately 50 percent of all marriages end in separation or divorce. What makes this story unique, though, is how this particular couple took the term *separation* to an entirely new level.

One day, after moving all of his belongings to one side of their home, the husband proceeded to chainsaw their house completely in half! The man then moved his half of the house to the opposite end of the property that the couple had also divided accordingly. Now they live on different sections of their property, each in their own half of the house. And then there was the man in England who, in an angry attempt to teach his ex-wife a lesson, neatly sawed every piece of furniture they owned in half. Then on one half of each of the couches, chairs, dressers, and beds, he spray-painted one word: *MINE*.

In addition to giving new meaning to the term *a house divided*, these drastic displays of anger and acts of revenge point to a much larger problem in many homes, marriages, and relationships in general: the inability to settle differences before irreparable harm is done. Do you think that, after forty years of marriage, the man in Cambodia suddenly woke up one morning, got mad at his wife for burning the toast, and took a chain saw to their house? No! Chances are some deep roots of bitterness had been neglected and given the chance to grow until that couple finally reached a breaking point. Too often we allow too much time to pass before settling our differences. And while some things in life—like an aged cheddar or a fine wine—grow sweeter with time, unresolved conflict is not one of them. If we allow the hours to turn into days, the days into weeks, and the weeks into months or years, chances are greater that, instead of understanding and forgiveness taking root, anger and resentment will grow. And, as Jesus taught long ago, "If a house is divided against itself, that house cannot stand" (Mark 3:25 NIV).

My parents never sawed *our* house in half. For this, I am grateful. But that does not mean that our walls never witnessed an argument. Far from it. Like all married people, my mother and father had their share of disagreements. What I witnessed as a child, though, was a mom and a dad who refused to stay mad for long. I think the most telling indication of how my parents chose to handle conflict came after I was already out of the house and about to get married myself. My parents each took turns offering up some words of wisdom that I, a scared kid getting ready to say, "I do," soaked up like a thirsty sponge.

One of the main pieces of advice I remember receiving was from my mother. She told me, "Never let the sun set on your anger." (Or, as the late comedienne Phyllis Diller put it, "Never go to bed mad. Stay up and fight.") My mom pointed me to the Scripture that she and Dad chose to live by when settling arguments: "Don't let the sun go down while you are still angry, for anger gives a foothold to the devil" (Ephesians 4:26–27). One definition of the word *foothold* is "a secure position from which further progress may be made." Anger left unattended is an open door for Satan to further his plan for your life, for your marriage, for your relationships. And make no mistake about it: Satan's plan for you is very different from the plan God has for you:

- **Satan** seeks to stir up resentment (Genesis 3:1);
  God desires reconciliation (Romans 14:19).
- **Satan** tries to fuel the fires of your anger (Proverbs 15:18);
  God desires peace (1 Corinthians 14:33).
- **Satan** wants to destroy your relationship (John 10:10);

God wants to rebuild your relationship and make it stronger than ever (1 Peter 3:8–9).

- **Satan** says you have the right to point a finger (Genesis 3:11–13);
  God leads you to examine yourselves first (Matthew 7:1–5).

At the point where conflict arises, we have two distinctly different paths to choose from. One leads to anger, resentment, and, ultimately, the tragic destruction of a relationship. The other leads to humility, reconciliation, and perhaps even a beautiful beginning to a lasting relationship.

I confess, though, that at different points in my life I have proudly marched down Satan's desired path, convinced that I was right and that reconciliation with the one who wronged me was simply not possible until he or she came to see our disagreement for what it really was: all his or her fault! And although I have never sawed a house in half or spray-painted furniture to prove a point, that word *MINE* has often been the cry of my heart and the only perspective I've been willing to see in a conflict. I have learned that, in some situations, no matter how hard I try, I simply can't see past my own nose. Sometimes it takes another person's perspective to help us get outside of ourselves.

I remember one sit-down with a trusted Christian counselor. That's right, I go to counseling. Funny, I grew up thinking there was this huge stigma about therapy. I would hear people in the church drop their volume to just above a whisper and say something like, "Oh, did you hear? So-and-so is in counseling." Somehow a person trying to turn a life or a relationship in a good direction had become good gossip. So I always used to think that counseling was for the people who were *really* screwed up, not for rational, clear thinking people like myself. Boy, was I wrong! I have come to realize the importance of seeking wise counsel to resolve conflict early in the process rather than waiting until the eleventh hour when the relationship is all but over. Besides, I'm convinced that people who recognize trouble spots early and are willing to humbly acknowledge their need for wise counsel will never wind up with a house chainsawed in half.

Not long ago my wife and I had hit a communication stalemate on a particular issue, and we needed an outside perspective to help us navigate the rough waters of our growing frustration. We each took turns sharing our side of the story with the counselor, and it was clear that we were on completely opposite sides of the issue, each believing we were right and the other person was wrong. The counselor kept quiet throughout most of our blaming. Then we both looked at him, waiting for him to crown a winner, but instead he said something very different: "I think it would be wise to begin as Jesus would have us begin. So, between now and our next meeting, I would like you both to take some time and think of two logs that may be in your own eye, two logs that may be impacting your perspective on this matter."

Ouch! That hurt a little bit. OK, OK, it hurt a lot. In that instant, though, I realized that never once during this disagreement had I even considered that I was at all responsible for any aspect of this conflict. How foolish of me! I also realized that I can be so self-absorbed that I am unwilling to examine myself— my attitudes, thoughts, motives, words, or actions. That is what my counselor was trying to get across. That is also what our Wonderful Counselor teaches all of us:

Why worry about a speck in your friend's eye when you have a log in your own? How can you think of saying to your friend, "Let me help you get rid of that speck in your eye," when you can't see past the log in your own eye? Hypocrite! First get rid of the log in your own eye; then you will see well enough to deal with the speck in your friend's eye. (Matthew 7:3–5)

Not every conflict can be settled in a day. But Scripture doesn't say, "Resolve all conflicts before the sun goes down." It says, "Don't let the sun go down while you are still angry." This is not an easy assignment, but it is essential to the process of conflict resolution and both to asking for and receiving forgiveness. In fact, one of the greatest defusers of anger is the humble realization that while there may be a speck in your friend's eye, odds are a log or two are in yours. So the next time anger arises, ask God to help you do some honest self-examination. Be humble enough to pray as David prayed: "Search me, O God, and know my heart . . . See if there is any offensive way in me, and lead me in the way everlasting" (Psalm 139:23–24 NIV). When both parties are praying that prayer, anger will subside, and forgiveness will be found.

JOSH

When I was growing up, my family was never much for verbal communication. Most of the time things would just go unspoken, and we would never really deal with issues that needed to be talked out. If one family member did or said something that hurt another family member, there was never an "I'm sorry." It was just assumed that the person was sorry. And because no one said, "I'm sorry," it was equally rare to hear the words "I forgive you." As a kid, I never knew any different, so I thought this was a normal way of dealing—or, actually, not dealing—with hurtful situations. We just moved on.

I'm married now and have a family of my own. And it took my wife to teach me the importance of communication, especially when it comes to disagreements and hurt feelings. One day we had an argument about something, and I said some hurtful words to her. She must have been able to tell that I was intending to just move on and either pretend it didn't happen or assume that she knew I was sorry. She stopped me and said,

"I know you're sorry, but it's important to speak that to me." So I looked her in the eyes and responded: "I'm sorry for what I said." Again, I thought that was the end of it. But she continued: "Now it's important for you to know that you are forgiven. I forgive you, Josh."

That day my wife taught me a valuable lesson I will never forget. I learned how important it is to speak an apology *and* speak forgiveness, not just feel those things. My wife has shown me that words are powerful, so I'm learning how to communicate with my family and friends in a way that keeps everything out in the open. I don't want to leave another "I'm sorry" or "I forgive you" unspoken. And I want my children to learn that from an early age by seeing how Mom and Dad communicate with each other even in disagreements.

⤳ SPEAK THE WORDS

Ever since I was kid, I've had a knack for watching a movie or TV show just once and then being able to repeat lines or even entire scenes. My dad always used to joke with me about this "skill." When I'd recite some goofy line from a funny movie, he'd say, "I wish you could quote the Bible the way you quote those movie lines!"

The movies, though, have provided us Wests with some pretty classic one-liners over the years. Some characters' lines have even woven their way into our everyday conversations. Who could forget a frightened young girl clutching her precious puppy as she ventured out into a scary new world saying, "Toto, I've got a feeling we're not in Kansas anymore." Or how about Jack Nicholson's character Colonel Nathan R. Jessep in the film *A Few Good Men*. This decorated military man takes the stand and faces fierce cross-examination in a high-pressured courtroom scene. The attorney demands that the colonel tell the truth, and good ol' Jack Nicholson fires back this legendary retort: "You can't handle the truth!" One of my favorite movies of all time is the classic *Cool Hand Luke*. It's the story of a man imprisoned in Florida who refuses to submit to authority. At one point the intimidating police captain says to the insubordinate inmate, "What we have here is a failure to communicate."

That line rings so true for so many of our relationships. It certainly applies to Josh's story. He himself described his family as one that had a "failure to communicate." Maybe yours does too. Maybe you come from a home where conflict was never resolved with an "I'm sorry" or an "I forgive you." Maybe you grew up understanding that some things were just better left unsaid, that an apology wasn't necessary. In many homes, so much has been swept under the rug over the years that family members have grown accustomed to walking around the mountain in the living room just to find the remote control. I know I would much rather leave that mountain alone most times and avoid conflict, especially if there's any chance I might wind up having to apologize to someone. I even rationalize my avoidance by thinking to myself, *Things just have a way of working themselves out sometimes.* But deep down I know that this line of reasoning is a coward's attempt to justify a conflict avoided or an apology left unspoken. After all, a real apology requires an uncomfortable combination of humility and courage. To really step up and resolve a conflict, I must be humble enough to admit when I'm wrong, yet brave enough to speak that truth out loud and ask for forgiveness.

The easy route is just to go around that mountain-covered rug, to choose a passive approach and hope that, magically, your family member or friend or coworker knows you're sorry without your having to say it. But the Bible gives us very different instructions: "Make every effort to live in peace with all men. . . . See to it that no one misses the grace of God and that no bitter root grows up to cause trouble and defile many" (Hebrews 12:14–15 NIV). Notice the charge to "make every effort." This is not the instruction to sit back and hope what's broken will fix itself on its own. No, throughout the Scriptures we find the clear challenge to be proactive in dealing with relationship conflict, whether we are the one who needs to apologize or the one who needs to forgive.

Furthermore, Jesus said, "If you are offering your gift at the altar and there remember that your brother has something against you, leave your gift there in front of the altar. First go and be reconciled to your brother; then come and offer your gift. Settle matters quickly with your adversary" (Matthew 5:23–25 NIV). Jesus didn't say, "Take your time to resolve a conflict." He said, "Go." Jesus didn't say, "Settle a grievance whenever you get around to it." He told us to settle our grievances "quickly." There is no promise that obeying these commands will be easy. In fact, it will most definitely be uncomfortable. But the Bible commands us to be quick to pursue reconciliation, and there must be a reason.

Josh knows the reason. Thanks to his wife, Josh now knows that in a healthy relationship, both people know where they stand; people communicate even when communication gets hard;

people refuse to let a "bitter root" grow; and, most importantly, neither is afraid to say, "I'm sorry." God wants you and me to have those kinds of relationships too. That is why these Scriptures instruct us to be proactive, speaking the words that must be spoken even when it would be easier simply to say nothing.

In the 1970 film *Love Story*, there is another famous movie line that applies to the importance of communication. During an intensely emotional conversation in one scene, the leading man is attempting to apologize to his love. With tears running down her face, the woman stops him mid-apology and says, "Stop it! Just stop it! Love means never having to say you're sorry." At first listen, those words sound right. But while they do wax poetic—like something you'd read on a greeting card—I think Josh would tell you that the message couldn't possibly be further from the truth. Love means *always* being willing to say you're sorry. Love means that we "make every effort to live in peace" with one another. It's time to stop walking around that mountain. The conflict isn't going to go away by itself.

But you can help make it go away by taking the first step toward the person who needs to hear you say, "I'm sorry." Or you can be the first one who climbs that mountain and lets someone hear a much-needed "I forgive you." You may be thinking to yourself, *It's just been too long* or *There's too much hurt* or *So many years have passed*. Regardless of where you are or how you've behaved or acted in a relationship up until this point, consider this a chance to start over. Handling conflict the way God wants you to is the first step to repairing and restoring even the most damaged relationship. Your efforts may even leave you and your former adversary quoting another famous Hollywood one-liner, this one by Humphrey Bogart in *Casablanca*. He turned to Louis with a smile and said, "I think this is the beginning of a beautiful friendship."

Stop sweeping the issue under the rug. Climb the mountain. Speak the words. And begin again.

WHEN FORGIVENESS WON'T COME

We were on a summer vacation in the mountains of Colorado last year, and our family time was nearing an end. On our last Saturday of vacation, my girls and I stepped into one of those tiny, touristy souvenir gift shops that every family visits on vacation. My daughter picked out a five-dollar ring that she wanted, and since one of my daughters liked it, that meant I would be purchasing two of these rings—one for her and one for her little sister. Turned out, these were not just ordinary rings. They were mood rings. Perhaps you are familiar with these mood-detecting devices. Supposedly, the ring changes color depending on the wearer's mood. Blue means happy, black means anxious, and so on and so on. Well, my daughters were fascinated by the thought of these rings changing colors every time their moods changed. I myself was curious to see if they could even begin to keep up with the many mood swings of my seven-year-old and four-year-old girls. I figured those rings would most likely change color about as often as the weather seemed to change up in that little mountain town: every hour on the hour. We exited the gift shop, hopped back into the car, and began driving back to our cabin in the woods. I couldn't help but listen in on the children's backseat conversation.

Lulu said, "Ooooh! Look! My ring turned blue, and if it's blue, that means I'm happy!"

Delaney, who only wants to be just like her big sister, said in a whining tone, "I want my ring to turn blue too. Why isn't my ring blue?"

Lulu thought for a second, and then making an effort to help her little sister, she offered her a seemingly sensible solution: "Well, hurry up and get happy and then your ring will turn blue!"

Don't you wish it were that easy?

"Hurry Up and Forgive Me!"

Lulu's good-hearted response of trying to rush her little sister into happiness reflects how I often respond to someone I have hurt. Only instead of my telling him to hurry up and get happy, I'm expecting him to hurry up and forgive me. After all, I said I was sorry. I've taken the steps I thought were necessary to mend the relationship, and now the ball is in his court. In fact, he is the only reason this relationship is not on the mend. I've done my part. I've asked for forgiveness, but he won't forgive. I can think of fewer more frustrating places to be than in a situation where you cannot make someone feel for you the way you want him to.

In an ideal world forgiveness would always go full circle. An apology would always be met with acceptance, enemies would stay enemies for only so long, and broken relationships would ultimately find healing and restoration. But you and I both know that's not always the case. Unfortunately, there will be times when our apologies fail to crack the surface of a heart that our hurtful ways or words have hardened. And we might find ourselves feeling helpless when we've gone as far as we can go to rebuild a bridge that has been burned only to realize that the bridge can't be constructed by just one person. Truth is, forgiveness—like happiness—is not a destination we can force another person to go to. That person must first be willing to move in our direction.

In the movie *Bruce Almighty*, actor Jim Carrey plays a down-on-his-luck news broadcaster with a "woe is me" attitude that has caused great strain on his relationship with his girlfriend, Grace. Bruce has hurt Grace time and time again, and eventually she decides she has had enough and must move on so her broken heart can heal. In a strangely irreverent twist, God confronts complaining Bruce and allows him to assume control for a while, granting him the power to change both his life and the world as he sees fit. Bruce falls in love with the newly found powers he has been given, but he ultimately winds up making a royal mess of everything because all of his "miracles" are guided by selfish ambition. He discovered that he could change the weather, he could change his job title, he could even change who won the lottery, but he couldn't change the way Grace felt about him. After several failed attempts to use his miracle-working powers to win Grace back, Bruce, in a candid conversation with God, asks, "How do you make someone love you without changing free will?" God replies, "Welcome to my world."

Are you grieving any broken relationships that have yet to come full circle because the other person is unwilling to forgive you? God has given to everyone else the same free will He gave you. We may grow impatient when someone is slow to accept our apology, yet we have no choice but to accept it as an opportunity to grow in our understanding of that person, our knowledge of ourselves, and our gratitude to God for His quickness to forgive us every time we fail.

Stepping Toward Forgiveness

Two steps in every twelve-step addiction recovery program address the issue of forgiveness. Step 8 encourages individuals to take "inventory," to make a list of all the people they have harmed: "We subjected ourselves to a drastic self-appraisal. Now we go out to our fellows and repair the damage done in the past. We attempt to sweep away the debris which has accumulated. . . ."[6] Then, next in the sequence, Step 9 directs individuals to write letters, to pay back debts, and to do and say whatever will help heal the hurt and repair the damage that they have done.

The twelve steps make it very clear that forgiveness may not always come and that, in some cases, forgiveness will not even be possible. But what I love about the twelve-step approach to forgiveness is the encouragement to focus on the only thing any of us can control—our own self! Step 9 says, "We need to be open to any response we get from people we've injured, and be ready to accept their response without becoming angry. We are not there to manipulate them into forgiving us. . . . We should make every effort to purge our bad feelings toward the person or incident before we meet to speak. This will help us resist the temptation to point out to them what we felt they did to provoke us. We are only there to talk about our own behavior."⁷

How difficult this step is for any one of us! Way too often, for instance, I have begun an apology with the purest intent, only to wind up weaving my own defense into the matter and, by doing so, rendering my apology absolutely meaningless. (Anybody know what I'm talking about?) If a particular relationship in your life has stalled out and failed to come full circle, I believe the instructions given in those two steps point to a very important key that is essential not only to those going through the twelve steps of recovery, but to everyone in need of learning the steps to take toward true forgiveness and the recovery of a relationship broken by hurt.

Have you done a "drastic self-appraisal"? Sure, you may have apologized to the person you wronged, but have you really attempted to put yourself in that person's shoes? Have you imagined how the same treatment might have made you react? Jesus said, "In everything, do to others what you would have them do to you" (Matthew 7:12 NIV). Is there any chance that the person you hurt feels that you aren't truly sorry for what you did? Is there any chance that you actually are *not* genuinely sorry for what you did? These are important questions that can only be asked if you are willing to step back from a broken relationship and do some honest self-appraisal.

Learn about such self-appraisal from King David and pray as he prayed: "Test my motives and my heart" (Psalm 26:2). When you find yourself at the end of an unfinished bridge, unable to build it the rest of the way, go back to the beginning. Start with yourself again. Be willing to subject yourself to that "drastic self-appraisal." Ask God to show you what your next step should be. Pray for the other person also. And remember that it is not an individual who completes the circle of forgiveness, but the One who made both of the individuals involved. God searches your heart and knows it well. He also knows the heart of the person on the other side of that great divide. And unlike the mood ring that will try its best to follow the mood swings of a six-year-old girl, God does not follow our moods. He alone is capable of bringing about real change in our lives and in our relationships, genuine change that lasts far longer than any mood. Don't give up. Instead, give Him your half of the circle of forgiveness. Bring Him your broken bridge. Whether or not the other person involved chooses forgiveness (there's that nasty free will again), you can know that "God causes everything to work together for the good of those who love God and are called according to his purpose for them" (Romans 8:28). You can also know that no relationship is too far beyond God's ability to rebuild: "What god is so great as our God? You are the God who performs miracles" (Psalm 77:13–14 NIV).

Maybe you need a miracle in a relationship today. But maybe you're the reason why you haven't received the forgiveness you desire. When forgiveness won't come, you know what to do. Go back to the beginning. Take God's hand and let Him help you retrace your steps. Let Him be more involved in your efforts to rebuild the bridge. Then rest in God's promise that He will bring good out of this hurt—that He will make you more like Christ— even if the person you hurt is not willing or able to work on completing the circle of forgiveness.

FORGIVING
YOURSELF

Show me how to love the unlovable
Show me how to reach the unreachable
Help me now to do the impossible

Forgiveness

JEREMY

I will never forget meeting Jeremy.

But first some of the backstory. As I travel in and out of cities across America, one nagging, recurring thought keeps me unsettled, some nights even as I hop on the stage: *I wonder how many people needed to be here tonight but couldn't come for one reason or another.* That thought has motivated me to reach out to children's homes, addiction recovery centers, and women's shelters in and near the cities I travel to and offer residents there the opportunity to attend. I must say, my interactions with these groups have been some of the most gratifying times in my ministry.

I remember one night before a show, I had the chance to spend a few moments with a group of young men from a nearby addiction recovery program. I was able to share a little bit of my heart with them and welcome them to the show. Jeremy caught my attention. He was young and handsome, all-American in appearance. His hair was neatly combed and his shirt tucked in (probably at the instruction of the center). If I hadn't known which group he came in with, I never would have guessed he was in recovery. He looked like he had the whole world of opportunity in front of him. In an effort to break the ice and connect with him, I started kidding around and said, "Hey, man! You better watch out. The girls are gonna be after you!" He looked up at me—and then right back down to the ground—saying, "No girl would ever want anything to do with an addict like me."

Jeremy's words fell heavy on my heart. I asked him to look at me. As he lifted his eyes, I asked God to give me an encouraging word to speak into his life in that moment. "Listen to me. That may be who you *were*, but that's not who you are anymore. You don't have to be owned by that."

I don't know where Jeremy is today. But I pray for him. I pray that these days he is holding his head a little higher, confident that God has not finished writing the story of his life.

JESUS STOOPED DOWN

I wonder what He was writing . . .

The Pharisees and the teachers of the law brought before Jesus a woman caught in the act of adultery. They asked Him

what He thought of the law that said she should be stoned for her actions. According to Scripture, Jesus' initial answer came in the form of an action: "Jesus stooped down and wrote in the dust with his finger" (John 8:6). There is no mention of what He wrote. No details about how long He stooped there or how many minutes He made the men attempting to trap Him wait while He carved this mystery message into the ground. And who was this message for? Was it one word or many? We don't know from Scripture exactly what He scribbled in the dust that day or to whom He was writing.

But as I picture that tension-filled scene, I think that Jesus' message in the dust was intended for one person and one person only. Let me explain. First, imagine the amount of shame that woman must have felt. Having been dragged into the temple court, she certainly wasn't holding her head high. Scripture says, "They put her in front of the crowd" (John 8:3). It wasn't enough for the Pharisees and teachers of the law to catch her in the act of adultery. They sought to humiliate her further, pushing her out in front of them and then backing up until she stood all by herself, the only divider between the crowd of accusers and Jesus. There she stood, closer to Jesus than to the Pharisees. Her sin exposed. Her family publicly disgraced. She was a pawn in the Pharisees' foolish attempt to trap Jesus.

She herself was trapped. She had nowhere to go, nowhere even to look. She wasn't about to face the Pharisees. You don't readily look in the eye of someone who wants you dead, and she wouldn't dare even to glance at the crowd Jesus had been teaching. Chances are she knew some of those people who were learning about her sin. And Jesus? How could she possibly lift her eyes to look at Him? After all, if the teachers of the law and the Pharisees were bringing her to see Jesus, she must have thought their accusations would pale in comparison to whatever judgment He might hand down. No, I imagine she hung her head in shame, looking down, staring at the dust. And Jesus "stooped." The Savior chose to send a message that only someone looking down at the dust would be able to read.

"They kept demanding an answer, so he stood up again and said, 'All right, but let the one who has never sinned throw the first stone!' Then he stooped down again and wrote in the dust" (John 8:7-8). Notice the emphasis on posture throughout the entire account of Jesus' actions as He faced the angry crowd and the humbled woman. Jesus stooped down, and then He stood up, and then once again He stooped down. Interesting, isn't it?

Jesus stood up to humble the high and mighty Pharisees, and He stooped down to lift up the lowly woman whose guilt kept her gazing down at the dust.

Perhaps the woman was surprised when she heard Jesus speak to the crowd in her defense, causing them to slip away one by one "until only Jesus was left in the middle of the crowd with the woman" (v. 9). But, then again, maybe she wasn't surprised. I wonder if those lines in the dust that only she could see had already delivered the message of mercy that her wounded heart so desperately needed. I love how the posture of Jesus changed one final time as He addressed the woman. "Then Jesus stood up again and said to the woman, 'Where are your accusers?'" (v. 10).

In the final recorded interaction between Jesus and the woman caught in adultery, He stood up to speak to her. By asking her where her accusers were, He was inviting her to look around and see that the coast was clear; they had all gone home. "'Didn't even one of them condemn you?' 'No, Lord,' she said" (vv. 10–11). And I imagine that, as He *stood* up, she *looked* up for the first time since this nightmarish event began. She lifted her head and stared straight into the eyes of compassion. She saw the kind face of One who cared enough to stoop down and send her a message of mercy where only she could see: on a pallet of dust.

With every passing second in the presence of forgiveness, the last remnants of her shame fell to that dirt floor where she had once fixed her gaze. But she wasn't looking down anymore—and she was amazed that not one stone had been thrown, not one person had condemned her. Then Jesus lifted the final weight from her heavy heart when He assured her, "Neither do I" (v. 11). Jesus stooped down, giving her the courage to stand up and start a new life by saying, "Go and sin no more" (v. 11).

There's a message for all of us written in that dust, for all of us who hang our heads, whose shame won't let us lift our eyes. We can see that message even if the crowd can't. We see the tracings of the Father left by the fingerprints of forgiveness. He stooped down to raise us up. We are not accused. We are not condemned. We are forgiven. And we are free to go forward now, holding our heads high and shaking the dust of the past from our feet. The dust where we once fixed our gaze. The dust where Jesus met us.

JORDAN

Hello, my name is Jordan, and I am a drug addict. That's how I introduced myself for the better part of four and a half years, and I had basically accepted that as my identity. I wasn't born or raised to be a drug addict. Quite the opposite, in fact. I was raised in a Baptist church where my father was the pastor and my uncle and grandfather were deacons. I was a three-sport athlete in high school: I played football and basketball, and I ran track. I was an all-state football player and a three-time state champion in track and field. I signed a scholarship to a Christian college in Kentucky where I also played football and ran track. College is where my life began to change. When I was a sophomore, I broke my ankle during a football game, and I was introduced to the prescription drug Oxycontin. I was immediately hooked.

I was a seven-time all-American in track in college, yet I was willing to give it all up for the drugs. I was able to stay in school and somehow play sports even though I was a full-blown drug addict—until my senior year in college. I failed a drug test, I was kicked off of the football team my senior year, and then I failed a second drug test. The second failed test got me a year-long suspension from both school and sports at Cumberland. During that year I was admitted to Cornerstone Recovery in Knoxville, Tennessee, and from there I was sent to Sandhills Teen Challenge in North Carolina. I struggled with so many things other than drug addiction, things I didn't even realize I had. The drugs had become a way to hide and escape from the real issues I was trying to avoid, including a relationship with Jesus Christ.

I was introduced to Christ as a child, but it was in my lowest valley that I truly came to understand what accepting Christ to be my Savior really meant. Grace is one of those things that you can't understand from the outside looking in, and I was forced to understand God's grace at that point because I had nowhere else to turn. I had lied to, stolen from, and hurt my family so badly that I could never imagine their wounds being healed, but they were.

For a long time I never thought I would be able to forgive myself. When I was in Teen Challenge, away from my family and friends, it was easy never to think about forgiving myself. It was easy not to worry about the guilt I actually felt and carried from my past. But when I went home and had to see my family and friends on a daily basis, I began to understand the pain and the scars I had caused because of my selfish decisions. And I struggled. Even though I had been in rehab and stayed clean for over a year, the pain and regret I felt were still very real. I continually referred to myself as a drug addict, and I always assumed people were talking about me or had a bad opinion of me or both. At one point it got so bad that my girlfriend at the time (my wife now) said, "Jordan, you're always gonna be a drug addict as long as you refer to yourself as a drug addict." And she was right. It took nearly two and a half years, but I believe I have finally forgiven myself for my past. I know the Lord forgave me a long, long time ago.

I graduated from Teen Challenge in December 2009, and the blessings keep coming. I recently finished my master's degree from the same college I was kicked out of. I have since married the love of my life, and I recently recognized and announced my calling to preach. I also am a teacher and coach at my high school alma mater. And I no longer introduce myself as a drug addict. Now I can say, "Hello, my name is Jordan, and I am a child of the one true King."

What's on your name tag? We all have one, you know. "Hello, my name is" and we fill in the blank. What we allow to be written on our name tag—or what we ourselves write—has the power to define how the world sees us, how we see the world, and, most significantly, how we see ourselves. For a long time Jordan chose to allow his poor choices and consequent battle with drug addiction to fill up the space on his name tag: "Hello, my name is Jordan, and I am a drug addict." Even after overcoming his addiction, he had a difficult time believing he could be defined by anything other than his shameful past and poor choices. Maybe you can relate.

Perhaps there are parts of your life that you are not proud of. And no matter how many times you attempt to erase those names on your name tag, you find yourself always returning to that old identity, believing that who you once were is who you are still and who you always will be. The great evangelist D. L. Moody wrote, "The voice of sin is loud, but the voice of forgiveness is louder." He's right. No matter how much time passes or how far away you may run from the past, sin can shout loudly enough to reach your ears and attempt to drag your heart right back to the place where you fell. Too many people spend too many days walking around with name tags that read "Shame," "Regret," "Failure," or "Lost Cause."

So, where can we turn to find our true identity? To our successes? Well, that might feel good for a little while. Who wouldn't want to have a name tag that points to a certain skill set or a special achievement? Jordan had that. Before he broke his ankle, his name tag read "Hello, my name is Jordan, and I'm an all-star athlete." But when that title was taken away from him, he was forced to search for a new identity. . . .

"Forgiveness is louder . . ." Greater than our greatest mistakes and even better than our best achievements is the message of God's forgiveness: it can drown out the voice of sin. And it is forgiveness that can once and for all lead us to see ourselves for who we really are. In fact, accepting God's forgiveness establishes a solid foundation for life:

- **Who we are NOT:** "We are no longer slaves to sin." (Romans 6:6)
- **Who we ARE:** "You are a chosen people, a royal priesthood, a holy nation, a people belonging to God, that you may declare the praises of him who called you out of darkness into his wonderful light." (1 Peter 2:9 NIV)

- **What we are CALLED**: "How great is the love the Father has lavished on us, that we should be called children of God!" (1 John 3:1 NIV)

When I had the honor of meeting Jordan in person, I asked him why he feels it is important not only to accept God's forgiveness but also to forgive oneself. This is what he told me: "One allows me to stand before God, holy and blameless. The other allows me to stand before man, fulfill my calling, and walk into my destiny without shame or guilt about my past. I was held captive by my past until I was able and willing to forgive myself. I was unable to move forward from my past because I was still a prisoner of my past."

Just like Jordan, you have been invited to walk into your destiny without shame or guilt. And just as Jordan experienced, the gift of forgiveness promises to erase those old names that you used to have on your name tag. Fill your heart and mind daily with reminders from Scripture that tell you the truth about who you are. And the next time those lies try to drag you down, you will be able to stand like Jordan and proudly proclaim, "Hello, my name is Child of the One True King!"

RUSTY

I grew up in a great Christian home, but decisions I made as a youth led me down a terrible road. During high school I experienced the death of two of my closest friends, and after their funerals I began to doubt God and question His existence. I quickly led others down the path I was on. One teacher stated in front of my classmates, "If my son grew up to be like you, I would kill myself." Addictions and criminal actions followed. I was expelled from school. I was blessed with a job after high school, but I quickly traded that in for a different job: dealing drugs. After I lost everything I found myself in cell number 121 in our local jail. I no longer had a name; I was an inmate with a number. I spent a year behind bars, and that year was filled with experiences no young man should ever have to endure. But it also turned into the best year of my life.

Behind bars I found my Savior, my Redeemer: I found Jesus Christ. He laid a vision on my heart to help the hurting, the homeless, and the addicted in our community. And while I was in jail, He gave me another number: 180. After I was released, I still faced the challenges of being a single father in my early twenties who was trying to live a Christian life. Some of my old friends and family abandoned me and threw me by the way-side because of my decision to follow Christ. And being a felon made it next to impossible for me to find a job. So I decided to follow the dream God put on my heart.

A year out of jail, when I was twenty-one, I started an orga-nization called The 180 Zone. I'm twenty-five now, and The 180 Zone has forty residential beds for homeless kids, teens, and families as well as addicted women and men. We also minister to about three thousand people every month through outreach programs. I decided to actually live in one of our facilities that houses men coming out of prison. I have lived there for three years now, and I wake up every morning to a dozen guys having a Bible study. Their tattoos and criminal records label them as hardened criminals, but listening to their Bible studies reminds me of the grace I have experienced in my life. Just four years earlier I was breaking into hotels for a place to stay. I remember waking up in my van homeless and with the worst feeling ever: hopelessness. Now, by the grace of God and His love, my mis-sion is to love people back to life and radically change our cities.

Forgiveness, to me, means a second chance at life. I've been in and out of the court systems since I was a teenager; I've paid thousands of dollars back in restitution trying to "make it right." But I could never do enough restitution in the world to make up for the pain I've caused. The idea that I'm forgiven is, honestly, unimaginable. I have been lost, but today I am found. I was found when God's forgiveness became a reality to me. I don't have to be an addict, homeless, or an inmate any longer. I am free to be Rusty, the person God created me to be. His forgiveness was the key to my freedom.

A NUMBER, A DONKEY, AND A NOT-SO-SUBTLE WAKE-UP CALL

When I first read Rusty's story, I thought of the apostle Paul. And whenever I think of Paul, I think of a donkey. And when I think of a donkey, I think of the word *stubborn*. And when I think of the word *stubborn*, I think of forgiveness. Did you follow all that? Let me back up a bit and explain.

Paul was a leading persecutor of the early Christians. He was a bad man who did bad things—and he didn't deny it either. In fact, Paul proclaimed it: "Christ Jesus came into the world to save sinners—of whom I am the worst" (1 Timothy 1:15 NIV). Like Paul, Rusty doesn't deny his past. He knows his rap sheet speaks for itself. He has lied, cheated, stolen, sold drugs, and hurt countless friends and family members along the way. God could have chosen to get Paul's and Rusty's attention any way He wanted to because, well, He is God. But sometimes the most stubborn people will only respond to a not-so-subtle wake-up call. Paul's wake-up call came during a long journey to Damascus when he was struck by a blinding light from heaven and knocked right off the donkey he was most likely riding on. "He fell to the ground and heard a voice saying to him, 'Saul! Saul! Why are you persecuting me?' 'Who are you, lord?' Saul asked. And the voice replied, 'I am Jesus, the one you are persecuting!'" (Acts 9:4–5).

Rusty's wake-up call came in a jail cell as he realized that he was no longer known by a name, but by his cell number. I'm sure Rusty had opportunities to heed the warnings of gentler wake-up calls before he woke up in jail. Maybe the warning came in a concerned phone call from his parents, a sit-down with a trusted friend, or even just a whisper of "Don't do it. You're heading down the wrong road" as he was about to commit one of his many crimes. I wonder if Paul heard a similar voice in his head right before he oversaw the stoning of a Christ follower. And I imagine that, like Rusty, Paul had his chances to make a change before he did. After all, God relentlessly pursues every heart. And, thankfully, He will do so by any means necessary, whether it means waking up in jail or being knocked off a donkey.

I have a friend who battled with drug addiction for years. I watched helplessly as his life continued to unravel with one bad choice after another, and I remember repeatedly thinking, "OK, this must be his rock bottom. Surely, this is the wake-up call that will get him to turn his life around." But, sadly, each time I thought he had hit rock bottom, the bottom would drop, and my friend would fall deeper. Unfortunately and, at the same time, fortunately, his wake-up call came in a form similar to Rusty's. My friend has been drug free for three years. Like Rusty and the apostle Paul, he found forgiveness the hard way—but he found it nonetheless.

So often, though, we are tempted to think that our past mistakes disqualify us from ever being used by God in the future. Post wake-up call, we may find ourselves so filled with shame about the choices we made that we miss a powerful truth waiting to be discovered in our "knocked off the donkey" experience.

The wake-up call—no matter how harsh it has to be—is a sign of God's pursuit of us. Think about it. If God had been done with Paul, why did He bother with the blinding light? But God *wasn't* done with Paul. God knew all of the bad Paul had done, yet still said this about him: "Saul is my chosen instrument to take my message to the Gentiles and to kings, as well as to the people of Israel" (Acts 9:15). God's plan for Paul was unfolding, and as a result of God's pursuit, one of the leading persecutors of early Christians went on to do more to shape Christianity than any other individual except Christ Himself. Similarly, Rusty has learned that God woke him up in that jail cell for a reason. He knows that, like Paul, he is God's "chosen instrument." And Rusty is walking in that truth every day as he watches how God uniquely uses his story to bring hope to hurting hearts at his shelter.

Our wake-up calls are proof that we have not and cannot outrun or out-wander the relentless, unstoppable, and, yes, stubborn love of the God who refuses to let us go. Jesus Himself promised us that security: "My Father, who has given them to Me, is greater than all; and no one is able to snatch them out of My Father's hand" (John 10:29 NKJV)." English poet Francis Thompson brilliantly described God as the "Hound of Heaven."

He does not pursue us only to withhold forgiveness from us. No, the Hound of Heaven matches your stubbornness with His patience, step for step, awaiting the day when you will wake up to the wonder of a new mission He has for you: to be a shining example to all the world that God's forgiveness can find even the most stubborn of hearts.

RONNIE

He says that Jesus died to take away my sins. He says I'm forgiven. I always tell him, "You couldn't understand, Pastor. You couldn't possibly understand."

I've been meeting with the preacher almost every week lately, and it really helps me while I'm there, but I walk out the door and feel the same old struggle. The preacher is always very encouraging to me, reminding me that God loves me no matter what I've done and showing me Scriptures to prove it, but in the back of my mind I'm thinking, *I wonder if he would say the same thing if he really knew all that I've done.* He knows about how I've messed up my family. He even knows I spent some time in jail. But there are some parts of my life that are just too hard for me to talk about, parts that nobody knows about except for me and God. And it's those parts of my life that I don't think I will ever be able to forgive myself for.

So how could God really love me? I don't even love me! In fact, if I'm being honest, I hate me. I hate who I became. And even though I'm trying to live a different life now than I used to, I can't seem to get past it. I can't seem to move on. I walk into church and just feel like a hypocrite, like I don't belong there. But something keeps me going back to those weekly meetings with the preacher. I want to believe that what he says is true. I'm trying to believe it. I think I do believe that God forgives me. But my guilt won't go away. It stays with me like a shadow, and it won't let me be free.

WHEN LOVING THE UNLOVABLE MEANS YOU

I think that if God forgives us we must forgive ourselves. Otherwise it is almost like setting up ourselves as a higher tribunal than Him.

C. S. Lewis[1]

Forgiveness often requires us to make a choice to love the unlovable. Always a difficult task. But what happens when the unlovable one we must forgive is staring back at us when we look in the mirror? The challenge of forgiving yourself can seem more impossible than forgiving someone else and even more difficult than believing that God could forgive you for mistakes you've made. The struggle to forgive ourselves seems to be Satan's last line of defense in his efforts to keep us held in the chains of unforgiveness. I may have found my way to forgive someone who wronged me. I may have found humility enough to ask for forgiveness from someone I have hurt. And I may have even opened my heart to the life-changing knowledge that grace is—just as Scripture says—"the gift of God" (Ephesians 2:8 NIV).

But as long as my eyes are focused on my failures and I remain disgusted by my past, forgiving myself will be out of the question, and so will the possibility of living life to the fullest. Guilt is a gravity-like force, powerful enough to push a soul down to the point where the gift of grace seems utterly unbelievable: "You couldn't understand. You couldn't possibly understand." These words were spoken by a soul who could not get past his past. Guilt can be so consuming that the remorse you feel for your mistakes makes it impossible for you to rejoice over all that God has offered to you in the cross and through Christ's sacrifice for your sins.

A Lesson from the Disciples

Remember the disciple Peter and how Jesus restored his life, forgiving him for his denial? And remember how Peter responded when he saw the resurrected Jesus standing on the shore and heard Jesus inviting him to breakfast? Peter jumped out of the fishing boat and swam to shore to greet the Lord. This action showed that Peter believed Jesus' forgiveness trumped any guilt he thought he deserved to carry.

But now consider the journey of Judas, a similar story with a much different ending. Judas betrayed Jesus as well, handing Jesus over to be crucified in exchange for thirty silver coins:

> When Judas, who had betrayed him, saw that Jesus was condemned, he was seized with remorse and returned the thirty silver coins to the chief priests and the elders. "I have sinned," he said, "for I have betrayed innocent blood."
>
> "What is that to us?" they replied. "That's your responsibility."
>
> So Judas threw the money into the temple and left. Then he went away and hanged himself. (Matthew 27:3–5 NIV)

Both disciples turned their backs on Jesus. Both were guilty of betrayal. Both were riddled with remorse and shame. But the two disciples allowed their guilt to drive them in vastly different directions. Peter hurried to accept Jesus' invitation to share breakfast together. It proved to be more than a meal. Jesus gave Peter the opportunity to wash away the guilt of his three denials by asking him three times, "Do you love me?" Peter answered yes each time. (John 21:7–17)

Judas, on the other hand, went to the wrong people and believed the wrong words—"That's *your* responsibility." The chief priests dug the dagger a little deeper into the wound of an already remorseful man who wished more than anything that he could undo what he had done. But, unlike Peter, Judas never found his restoration. And ultimately the weight of responsibility—being told the guilt for his treachery was his burden alone to bear—proved too heavy to carry. Jesus died on a cross for the responsibility Judas felt. Yes, it was Judas's sin that put Jesus there. It was my sin that put Him there. It was Ronnie's sin. And it was yours too. But because of our Savior's selfless sacrifice, the responsibility for our sin is no longer ours to carry. It has been carried for us. Carried far, far away. "He has removed our sins as far from us as the east is from the west" (Psalm 103:12).

Do you think Peter was ever able to fully forget that night by the fire when he could have stood up for his Friend but instead denied knowing Him? Well, if Peter was anything like me, I bet he never forgot. I remember my failures. I have a feeling you remember yours too. The key to forgiving yourself is not to forget, but to allow God to change how you remember.

Changing How You Remember

After all, I do not believe that "forgive and forget" is the goal of any aspect of forgiveness. Lewis B. Smedes wrote, "Forgiving does not erase the bitter past. A healed memory is not a deleted memory. Instead, forgiving what we cannot forget creates a new way to remember. We change the memory of our past into a hope for our future."[2]

Jesus wanted Peter to know that there was a future for him beyond his betrayal. Jesus helped Peter see that his life still had purpose, that God wasn't done with him yet when He said, "Feed my sheep" (John 21:17). Jesus' command to Peter was infused with purpose, and it sent the message to Peter that it was time to move on, time to get back to the business of being used by God. And that is exactly what Peter did. Forgiven and freed, Peter went on to do great things just as the other disciples did. He became one of the pillars of the early church, and on the day of Pentecost, he preached these passionate words:

> "Each of you must repent of your sins and turn to God, and be baptized in the name of Jesus Christ for the forgiveness of your sins. Then you will receive the gift of the Holy Spirit. This promise is to you, and to your children, and even to the Gentiles—all who have been called by the Lord our God." (Acts 2:38–39)

Scripture says that about three thousand people were saved that day. Peter had indeed responded to Jesus' challenge to move on, and Peter fed Jesus' sheep.

But there is no way Peter would have been able to stand before the crowd and preach that message if he were still weighed down by self-loathing and guilt. No, Peter had been given the opportunity to see himself as Jesus saw him. When we struggle to forgive ourselves, we too often look at our reflection and see *unlovable*. Jesus, however, sees *unfinished*. Max Lucado wrote, "God loves you just the way you are, but he refuses to leave you that way. He wants you to be just like Jesus."[3]

Maybe right about now you're feeling like Ronnie who wrote about his struggle at the beginning of this chapter: *You just don't understand.* Well, Jesus understood Peter. He understood Judas. And He understands you. You may see yourself as unlovable, but God doesn't. Believe that what His Word says is true: "There is now no condemnation for those who are in Christ Jesus" (Romans 8:1 NIV). No matter how unlovable you feel, you are loved. Don't ask God to help you forget your past. Ask Him to help you remember the past in a new way and embrace the freedom of "no condemnation." Do this and then be prepared for God to use you—just as He used Peter—to reach an entire world of people outside your door who think they are unlovable too.

EMBRACING GOD'S FORGIVENESS

It'll clear the bitterness away
It can even set a prisoner free
There is no end to what it's power can do

So let it go and be amazed
By what you see through eyes of grace
The prisoner that it really frees is you

Forgiveness

GINNY

One of the worst decisions I ever made was when I was eighteen: I became pregnant and decided to get an abortion. I was too afraid and ashamed to go to my parents for help, so I decided to fix my mistake and terminate the pregnancy. Marriage was not an option for me because I knew I did not love my boyfriend enough to marry him. I still remember climbing the stairs in the clinic with a group of other young women.

The experience was so much more painful than I expected, because it was not only physical pain. I have always been sorry that I did not seek out other options, and I have often thought about how different my life would be if I had chosen to give life. Taking the life of my child was unforgivable in my eyes, so from that point on I tried to earn God's forgiveness.

That was thirty-five years ago. But today I have hope! When I finally listened to God's Word, I discovered that I could not earn forgiveness. I simply needed to accept that Jesus' death on the cross covered all of my sins—past, present, and future. He really does love me, no matter what I've done. I know that God has forgiven me and that I will meet my child in heaven one day. I made a poor choice in 1975, but today I have hope and a strong desire to lead children to Christ at an early age so I work with children's ministries at my church.

It's hard to describe the feeling of being free from secrets. I have no more fear or shame. The chains of bondage have dropped. The voice of lies has been silenced. The wall of darkness has fallen. I can see His beauty. Even my friends say they can see a difference in me. I have given my story of abortion over to Jesus and have made a commitment to reach out to others who are held in this dark bondage of Satan's lie that your secret is something God won't forgive.

✳ A LIFETIME OF SECRETS

I recently stumbled upon a fascinating book entitled *A Lifetime of Secrets*. What began as an art project for Frank Warren turned into this *New York Times* best seller collection of, well, secrets. Warren gave people of all backgrounds and

nationalities a chance to set their secrets free by writing them down on a postcard and sending them to him. The book's pages are filled with postcard after postcard, each revealing a secret that someone needed to tell. Some secrets are humorous, like the one printed on the back of a Starbucks cup, evidently by an employee, confessing, "I give decaf to customers who are rude to me!" Other secrets dug deeper, revealing real hurt, real pain, or real insecurities like this one that read, "I smile all the time so that nobody knows how sad and lonely I really am."[1] Some people had a different type of secret to tell. The kind of secret we keep in hopes of hiding the shame and guilt we feel because of past mistakes. Secrets like Ginny's.

When I first read her story, I had no idea that she, in fact, was actually revealing a secret. A secret she had kept even from those closest to her for thirty-five years. When I called her to inform her that her story had inspired me to write a song called "The Healing Has Begun," I discovered how really difficult it had been for her to write down her story and send it to me. I asked her, "Ginny, why me? After all these years of keeping your abortion a secret, why did you choose to share your secret with me?" She responded with a laugh and said, "Well, I never thought you'd actually read it!" She continued, "But I'm so glad that you did. Because now I have nothing to hide, and I feel free for the first time in a long time."

Ginny went on to describe to me what happened on the day she sat down to write her story. She said at first she began writing about another painful chapter in her life, her parents' divorce. But something made her stop. And suddenly this question entered her mind: *What is it really? What is that one part of your story that has kept you from feeling free, from experiencing the close relationship with God that you desire?* Ginny said that is when she knew it was time. Time to set her secret free.

When you see or hear the word *secret*, what comes to mind? Is there a part of your life—maybe a mistake you made or something that happened to you that brought much shame—that you've never shared with anyone? Nothing can drive a heart to seek shelter in the shadows like shame can. It's the feeling that comes when the light of day shines brightly on what you did, when the fog of confusion that clouded your judgment lifts, and you see all too clearly the mistake you've made and will always regret. Maybe you've reached a point when you were so disgusted with yourself you thought, *What I have done is so terrible, so wrong, no one can ever know. No one!* And so a secret is born.

But while we may succeed in keeping our secrets hidden

from friends, family, and even our spouse, there is One for whom our secrets are no surprise. The Creator of the universe is well aware of every single detail of our life—the good, the bad, even the ugly. He knows our deepest secrets.

- **He sees all things.** "My eyes are on all their ways; they are not hidden from me, nor is their sin concealed from my eyes." (Jeremiah 16:17 NIV)
- **He knows all things.** "Before a word is on my tongue you know it completely, O LORD." (Psalm 139:4 NIV)
- **He reveals all things.** "He reveals deep and hidden things; he knows what lies in darkness, and light dwells with him." (Daniel 2:22 NIV)

Every thought you've ever thought. Every lie you've ever told. Every moment when it seemed no one was looking. God sees all things, knows all things, and reveals all things. If I'm being honest, part of me finds that truth to be a scary realization. But Scripture shows that there is not fear but freedom in knowing and being known by an all-knowing God. One of the clearest pictures of this is found in John 4 when Jesus meets the Samaritan woman at the well. Now, believing that Jesus knows all things leads us to the conclusion that He was not simply resting at Jacob's well by happenstance when the woman came to draw water. What He revealed to her during their conversation at the well was further proof of His intentionality, and their encounter would change her life:

> Jesus replied, "Anyone who drinks this water will soon become thirsty again. But those who drink the water I give will never be thirsty again. It becomes a fresh, bubbling spring within them, giving them eternal life."
>
> "Please, sir," the woman said, "give me this water! Then I'll never be thirsty again, and I won't have to come here to get water."
>
> "Go and get your husband," Jesus told her.
>
> "I don't have a husband," the woman replied.
>
> Jesus said, "You're right! You don't have a husband—for you have had five husbands, and you aren't even married to the man you're living with now. You certainly spoke the truth!" (John 4:13–18)

In an instant, during what initially appeared to be a chance meeting with a stranger at a well, every single one of this woman's secrets was brought to light. And notice how she handled it:

"Sir," the woman said, "you must be a prophet. So tell me, why is it that you Jews insist that Jerusalem is the only place of worship, while we Samaritans claim it is here at Mount Gerzim, where our ancestors worshiped?" (John 4:19–20)

The woman attempted to change the subject! Perhaps she had grown so accustomed to a life of shameful secrets that she somehow thought, *If I bring up a new topic, maybe my personal life can hurry back to the shadows where it is safer.* But Jesus continued to speak truth into her life, ultimately proclaiming, "I Am the Messiah!" (John 4:26). And I love what the woman did next:

> The woman left her water jar beside the well and ran back to the village, telling everyone, "Come and see a man who told me everything I ever did! Could he possibly be the Messiah?" So the people came streaming from the village to see him. (John 4:28–30)

Jesus the Messiah knew all about the woman's failed personal relationships. He knew about Ginny's abortion thirty-five years ago. And He knows your secrets too. And just like the woman at the well and just like Ginny, you can be released from the burden of shameful secrets you carry. When we keep secrets, we are revealing our doubt that God could see us at our very worst and still offer us His forgiveness and love. But the woman at the well came face-to-face with the Savior who saw her secrets and still offered her "living water" (John 4:10). And what did she do? She ran back home shouting, "Come and see a man who told me everything I ever did!" God replaced her fear with freedom—and He can do the same for you. Set your secret free. Your Father in heaven already knows it anyway. So talk to Him today. Acknowledge that you know He knows and ask Him to lead you into the light of forgiveness, a light that can shine away the last shadows of your shame.

NOT ANOTHER KNOT

We learn the rope of life by untying its knots.

Jean Toomer

I've got a bucket list. I've never actually written it down, but I have one. And if you've ever found yourself saying, "I've always wanted to do that," then you have a bucket list too, and whatever "that" is, is on the list.

I've always wanted to go fly-fishing. But since I'm a city boy, activities that involved the great outdoors have eluded me most of my life. My dad raised me with a baseball glove and bat in my hands, not a fishing pole. Instead of wading in a river, we were exploring the concrete jungle of downtown Chicago. The closest I ever got to being one with nature was at Wrigley Field cheering on the Cubs, smelling that fresh-cut grass, and gazing at the beauty of those outfield walls covered with ivy. So, yeah, we were never the outdoorsy type. Up until last summer, fly-fishing had yet to be checked off the ol' bucket list.

My friend John, on the other hand, is an avid fisherman, and he invited me to join him for a day of fly-fishing on the Roaring Fork River in Colorado. John is no stranger to these legendary waters, and those fish are no strangers to the hook at the end of his line. And thanks to John I was about to cross this long-standing item off my bucket list.

I could hardly sleep the night before our trip as I envisioned the quiet, calm serenity of a day rolling down the river. I pictured myself casting the line with such grace and ease that even the fish would marvel at my movement, pure poetry in motion, and find my lures absolutely irresistible. In my mind I saw trout jumping out of the water, fighting over which one would get caught. I was sure I would catch even more fish than the disciples caught when Jesus told them to try the right side of the boat. The mayhem that unfolded that next morning, however, looked nothing like my dreams from the night before.

Knots. I caught knots. And that's about the only thing I caught the whole day. I'm not sure what went wrong. After all, our guide had given me a crash course in how to cast just before we headed down the river. He told me how the thing-a-ma-bobber attaches to the jig-a-ma-what-y. I heard something about keeping my elbow still, or was I supposed to raise it above my head? Needless to say, somewhere between the shore and the boat, I forgot every single thing he taught me. And to make matters worse, I could tell that our guide was in a grumpy mood. It was clear that he had spent years fishing this river, and his patience with beginners like me was pretty much spent.

As we headed down the river, I sat in the back of the boat, let my line go, and slowly began to reel it in. No fish. So I reached back and cast my line with all the precision of a blindfolded first-grader attempting to pin the tail on the donkey, and before I even had a chance to catch a fish, my line was tangled. Unbelievable! We had just started fishing, and I was already in trouble! I don't know how it happened. Maybe it was the elbow thing I couldn't remember. But I wasn't about to confess to my grumpy guide that I had a knot. No way!

Instead, I sat quietly in the back of the boat while we floated down the river and attempted to untie the knot on my own. What did I get for my efforts? More knots. Within minutes I had made a royal mess of my entire fishing pole. There were knots upon knots. And then there were knots upon knots upon knots! And that's when I did catch one thing as I sat in the back of that boat—my shorts! Now, I know someone once said that a bad day of fishing is better than a good day of work. Sitting in the backseat of the boat with a hook holding my shorts hostage, I wasn't so sure about that.

Finally, with my head hanging in shame, I broke down and spoke up. "Excuse me, sir.... umm ... I ... umm.... I seem to have a bit of a problem here," I confessed to the grumpy guide. Just as I'd been afraid of, the guide huffed and puffed as he guided the boat to shore. All I could think about was the fact that I was responsible for every minute we were spending *not* catching fish. Our guide did little to make me feel otherwise. Instead, he squinted at my poor excuse for a fishing line, shook his head in disgust, and asked a question I knew he didn't want me to answer, "Son, what in the world did you do?" I was wondering the same thing.

Sometimes my life feels a lot like my fishing line looked during that frustrating day on the river. A little snag, a mistake, a struggle, a lie, or an unconfessed sin left in my own hands can quickly turn into a fist full of knots seemingly too tangled for me to untie. How do I get myself so tangled up?

Then, as if the tangles weren't trouble enough, just as I was afraid to go to my river guide for help, I am often equally afraid to go to God. No matter how many times I've heard about a heavenly Father who loves and forgives and saves, I still struggle with the fear that if I were to present my knots to God, I might be met with the same disappointed, frustrated, head-shaking response with which my huffing and puffing grumpy guide reacted to my tangled mess of a fishing line. After all, God has given me all the instructions for how I am supposed to live. I go to church. I read the Bible. And yet at some point after Sunday morning, at some point as the week unfolds, I forget how to do it right. So I sit in the back of the boat and quietly convince myself that it is safer and easier to find my own way out of the mess I'm in—and the number of knots piles up.

It's funny. Our knots are often what keep us from going to God, but those knots are the very reason why God came to us in the first place. Jesus said, "It is not the healthy who need a doctor, but the sick. I have not come to call the righteous, but sinners" (Mark 2:17 NIV). If I were already an expert fly fisherman, I would have no need for a guide. And if I were without sin, without knots, I would have no need for a Savior. But perfect is one thing I'm not. Nobody is. And no matter how we may try, it is impossible to untie the knots of sin in our lives without help.

God is well aware of our knots, and Scripture offers this encouragement for how to handle them:

"Let us throw off everything that hinders and the sin that so easily entangles, and let us run with perseverance the race marked out for us. Let us fix our eyes on Jesus, the author and perfecter of our faith, who for the joy set before him endured the cross, scorning its shame, and sat down at the right hand of the throne of God" (Hebrews 12:1–2 NIV).

I love how Paul urged us to "fix our eyes on Jesus." Our sin tempts us to turn our eyes away from Jesus, but we must choose to look to Him instead. We must go to our Guide. He who is the "author and perfecter of our faith" is the One who can help us untie the knots of "sin that so easily entangles." There is forgiveness in that promise. And there is freedom in that forgiveness.

In case you're wondering if that first frustrating fly-fishing trip was also my last, the answer is no. I phoned my friend John and told him I wanted to try again. Only this time we took to the mighty river with a different guide. From the minute we met J.P., I could tell this was going to be a much more laid-back experience. "Dude, let's go catch some monstro toads, dude!" (Yes, he did say *dude* twice in the same sentence—and about five thousand more times that afternoon.)

I eventually gathered that *monstro toads* was J.P.'s term for "monster fish." At any rate, our surfer-dude-turned-fishing-guide made me feel relaxed and at ease from the second we pushed away from shore. His positive attitude made all of the pressure of doing something you're not very good at disappear. Did I still get tied up in knots? You betcha! But this time I wasn't afraid to tell my forgiving guide about it because I knew that instead of being met with a scowl, I would be met with a smile. I knew that my guide knew what he was there for: to untie my knots, to help me, to get me back out on the water to catch some fish. And boy, did we catch some fish! I caught one that was *this big*... (OK, OK, I'll quit while I'm ahead...)

Like my guide J.P., your Guide knows about your knots. He's the only One who can untie them and get you back to running the race that has been marked out for you. Perhaps it's time to trust in the goodness of your Guide and lift your knots up to Him. Let your heavenly Father's hands of forgiveness handle your knots, and your sin will entangle you no more.

SAM

Where do I start? At twenty-one I got a girl I barely knew pregnant and felt the right thing to do was to marry her. We had another child soon after. Four years later, we were fighting all the time. There never really was any love in our marriage. We divorced. I married another woman who had children of her own. I wound up neglecting my own children and taking care of hers instead. I rarely paid child support and only saw my own children on occasion. This reality is hard for me to look at as these words appear on the page. Now, here I am thirty years later. Alone.

My second wife left me for another man. I barely hear from my stepchildren, and I am sure my own children still carry the scars from my neglect. We just never talk about it. I battle with depression now. Spend the holidays alone. I'm just so ashamed of the mess I have made of my life. There's a part of me that aches to believe something good—anything good—could still come of the time I have left on earth. But these days the regrets from my past seem to be the only thing I can carry into the future. I feel like it's too late for me to make a mark. Too late to leave a legacy.

IT'S NOT TOO LATE

Jesus, remember me when you come into your Kingdom.

Luke 23:42

We never find out where he came from. There are no pages, not even a single paragraph, telling of his younger years or what his family was like. The final chapter of his story is the only one recorded. We never even learn his name. We know him only as the thief on the cross, one of the two guilty criminals crucified next to the innocent Jesus.

But surely this man must have seen better days. Even the most evil of criminals who commit the vilest *offenses* start out as *defenseless*, innocent children who have their whole lives in front of them. No one can pick out a future criminal by looking at baby photos. Maybe this criminal loved to run and play. Maybe he had freckles on his face and a smile that could light up any room. Maybe he always knew how to make his brothers laugh. Perhaps he loved to follow his dad to work or cuddle up next to his mommy before bedtime.

Sure, we know who he became, but we know nothing of how he got there. Did a traumatic experience in his youth send his life spinning out of control? Was he orphaned as a child and forced to fend for himself at a young age? Or did he simply make one bad choice after another, eventually slipping further and further away from the innocence he once knew? He now bore absolutely no resemblance to that freckle-faced kid with a bright future. Three nails and a cross had sealed his fate; he was paying the ultimate price for the crimes he had committed. And those crimes must have been awful because crucifixion was the form of punishment reserved for the worst of criminals. This man hanging next to Jesus was the equivalent of today's death row inmates waiting to die for what they have done.

I am sure you have heard someone after narrowly escaping a potentially dangerous or fearful situation exclaim, "I just saw my whole life flash before my eyes!" Maybe you've said that yourself. It's a common cliché we hear spoken when someone faces what is felt to be a near-death experience. I wonder if the thief on the cross experienced that. Perhaps in the midst of his excruciatingly painful punishment, his mind wandered back to those days of innocence.

Back to the feel of his mother's lips on his cheek.

Back to the laughter of his siblings.

Back to the proud embrace of his father after a chore done well.

I imagine that, in his mind, this criminal retraced all that had led up to his first mistake, his first crime, his first taste of guilt and regret. I imagine that, as he hung dying on his cross, he wished more than anything that he could go back and undo all the wrong he had done. I imagine this because of the way he chose to spend his final breaths. Speaking to the other criminal hanging next to him, this man said, "Don't you fear God even when you have been sentenced to die? We deserve to die for our crimes, but this man hasn't done anything wrong" (Luke 23:40–41). This thief stood up to the other criminal who was hurling insults at Jesus.

Quite out of character, don't you think? This man who had done so much wrong in his life was now finishing the final chapter of his story in a different light. But why? Perhaps, as his whole life flashed before his eyes, he wondered, *What happened to me? How did I get here? Where did my innocence go? I know right from wrong. Oh, how I wish I could go back.* Perhaps seeing an opportunity to prove that he did indeed know right from wrong, he took up for Jesus and, in doing so, offered a brief glimpse of the innocence that his earlier chapters may have known.

Then he made this request of the Messiah: "Jesus, remember me when you come into your Kingdom" (Luke 23:42). Pretty bold, don't you think? I mean, did this thief actually believe he could skate into heaven at the very last moment? Was it realistic to think this single honorable gesture to defend Jesus could blot out the laundry list of offenses that had landed him on a cross in the first place? Yes. That is exactly what he hoped for—but what he received was so much more.

In Jesus' presence, the thief on the cross became a different man. His hardened criminal's heart softened. He took up for Jesus—and then he dared to ask Jesus to take him up. The Scriptures encourage us to "come boldly to the throne of our gracious God. There we will receive his mercy, and we will find grace to help us when we need it most" (Hebrews 4:16). Never had the thief on the cross needed grace more than during his last dying breaths. And Jesus gave it to him: "I assure you, today you will be with me in paradise" (Luke 23:43).

Was it the way the thief defended Jesus that prompted the Savior to bless him with the promise of paradise? No. Jesus wasn't waiting for a good deed. Brennan Manning wrote, "My deepest awareness of myself is that I am deeply loved by Jesus Christ and I have done nothing to earn it or deserve it."[2] As the thief saw his entire life flash before his eyes, Jesus saw it too. The Savior could retrace the thief's steps as well as the thief himself could. And Jesus can retrace yours too, as the psalmist understood: "All the days ordained for me were written in your book before one of them came to be" (Psalm 139:16 NIV). Jesus doesn't wait for us to do something good enough to outweigh the bad we've done and then offer us paradise. He simply waits for us to accept His invitation and "come boldly to the throne of our gracious God" (Hebrews 4:16). Then not only will He remember us, as the thief humbly requested, but He will be *with* us—and we will be with Him—in paradise.

It wasn't too late for the thief on the cross to find forgiveness. It's not too late for Sam. And it's not too late for you. But what we must learn from the thief on the cross is that there is no trying involved in forgiveness. There is nothing we can do; there is no good deed that will make forgiveness any more attainable than our Father has already made it. We are simply called to ask for and then receive the free gift of grace.

In light of that truth, I guess it is fitting that the Bible only records this one pivotal moment in the thief's life. Scripture doesn't bother to include his laundry list of sins, and Jesus doesn't bother reading yours. He died for that list and made this promise: "I—yes, I alone—will blot out your sins for my own sake and will never think of them again" (Isaiah 43:25).

Maybe you can relate to Sam. Maybe you're thinking it's too late for you—and Satan would love for you to believe that. He is "the father of lies" (John 8:44), and he knows that if he can get you to believe the lie that it's too late for you, then your future will be nothing more than a reflection of a regretted past. But Jesus said, "I have come that they may have life, and have it to the full" (John 10:10 NIV). He did not say, "I came so that people could have life to the full, but it's too late for you, because you blew it." Instead, Jesus offers us "life to the full" starting right here and now, in this very moment. If your heart is beating . . . if there's breath in your lungs . . . it's not too late. In his final seconds on earth, the thief on the cross tasted life to the full and received the promise of paradise forever.

How will the rest of your story go?

FORGIVENESS FOR ALL

I came across an interesting online article this morning. The headline read "38 Stars Who Were Arrested in 2012." My curiosity compelled me to click on the link. The article showed some of our beloved Hollywood A-listers, B-listers, even C-listers in a less than flattering light. We've seen them in movies. We've listened to their music. We've celebrated their athletic accomplishments. This time, however, they were posing for mug shots. One celeb was sporting a brand-new black eye from a barroom brawl. Another looked as if she hadn't showered in a year. And with each unflattering profile picture, a detailed description of their indiscretions was published for all to see. Our celebrities may have grown accustomed to living above the law, but in these particular instances, the law won. There were stories of drunk driving charges, drug possession, tax evasion. And the list went on. These celebrities seemingly had everything life can offer, but they apparently wanted more. And now they were paying the price.

A very public price, I would add. As if it's not enough that these high-profile celebrities have been busted by the police, then the whole world is given a front-row seat from which to watch their weakest moments play out like a bad reality TV show. With the manner in which media covers this news it would appear that we, the public, certainly do love to see our celebrities fall. We build larger-than-life heroes, put enviable icons on pedestals, and imagine beautiful people with pristine personas. Then we spy on them, following their every move, just waiting for them to slip. When that happens, those magazines that plaster these celebrity images on their covers, bragging about their beauty or abilities, don't hesitate to put them on display again, but for a much different reason.

The religious community has its celebrities as well, and I have witnessed some of the harshest judgment ever from fellow believers who have misbehaved. More than a few celebrity Christians, ministers of megachurches, big-name gospel singers, and charismatic television evangelists have made a mistake, fallen short of perfection, and paid a painfully public price. And every time this occurs, we Christians appear shocked, stunned, disappointed, and appalled by the revelation that even the celebrity Christians are, as the old hymn says, "prone to wander." This is my point: Sin levels the playing field. Sin humbles the superhuman. When it comes to shortcomings, the scales between white collar and blue, between celebrity and noncelebrity, balance out in a hurry.

Maybe as you read this, you are thinking, *I'm far from famous. What does this have to do with me*? The truth is, celebrities are just like everybody else. Whether you are a professional athlete or a professional plumber, you can add another title to your resume: sinner. "For *all* have sinned and fall short of the glory of God" (Romans 3:23 NIV, emphasis added). If you've ever thought you have nothing in common with a celebrity, now you know you do. And as much as you might wish that what you had in common is the amount of cash they have in a bank account or the villa they own in Tuscany, it's a far less desirable similarity you share. It's sin. We all sin. We all struggle. We all wander from God's way. We all need forgiveness. And God offers a solution that is just as inclusive as the sinful nature that plagues us all.

Even King David

I think of King David as one of the first celebrities in history. This guy could do no wrong—or so it seemed. Take down a bear? Easy. How about a lion? Sure. Kill a giant named Goliath that everyone else in the land was afraid to face? No problem. Become the king of Israel? Done. Have your pick of the most beautiful women in all the land? Can you say "Bathsheba"? And I would call King David a rock star if only the Bible had left out the little detail that he played a harp. (That's not really a rock star instrument.) But on all other counts, David had clearly surpassed his shepherd status and exchanged it for royalty. Scripture says, "The LORD gave David victory everywhere he went" (1 Chronicles 18:13 NIV).

Yet even David—the only person in the Bible described as "a man after God's own heart"—could not escape the *all* in "For *all* have sinned." And like the celebrities featured in the article I read this morning, his weaknesses and sins have been recorded for all to see. The Bible's detailed description of David's indiscretions reminds us that not even a man after God's own heart is beyond needing God's forgiveness. Not only are we given a window into David's world as it shattered around him because of sin, but we also have the chance to gain great insight from his journey to forgiveness. Psalm 51 captures this fallen man's earnest prayer as he comes to grips with his sins of adultery and murder. "Have mercy on me, O

God, because of your unfailing love. Because of your great compassion, blot out the stain of my sins" (Psalm 51:1). In many other psalms a forgiven David sang the praises of the God who saved him: "Let all that I am praise the LORD; may I never forget the good things he does for me. He forgives all my sins" (Psalm 103:2–3).

David's prayer is proof that even though he was king, he knew he did not possess the power to meet his greatest need: David needed forgiveness. The same is true for me. The same is true for you. Everyone from the highest of us to the lowest, from the richest to the poorest, from the most well-known to the least known—"*all* have sinned." Nobody is able to avoid sinning; no one is able to free himself from the consequences of sin. And nobody has to be bound by those consequences either.

The Bible erases the *less* from the word *hopeless*. God's Word makes no mistake about the seriousness of our sin—"For the wages of sin is death"—but Scripture also presents the solution: "the free gift of God is eternal life through Christ Jesus our Lord" (Romans 6:23). And this solution is not only for a select few. God's grace goes out to the same *all* who have sinned. Read these Scriptures and notice their inclusive language (emphasis added):

- "Come to me, *all* of you who are weary and carry heavy burdens, and I will give you rest." (Matthew 11:28)
- "God so loved *the world* that he gave his one and only Son, that *whoever* believes in Him shall not perish but have eternal life." (John 3:16 NIV)
- To *each one of us* grace has been given as Christ apportioned it. (Ephesians 4:7 NIV)

All of us have sinned. *All* of us have been offered forgiveness by God. And one day *all* of us will stand before Him.

- We must *all* appear before the judgment seat of Christ. (2 Corinthians 5:10 NIV)
- At the name of Jesus *every* knee should bow, in heaven and on earth and under the earth, and every tongue confess that Jesus Christ is Lord. (Philippians 2:10-11)

Hopefully, you will never have to know how it feels for your sins to be on display for the world to see. And you'll never see your mug shot printed in the pages of a magazine or your private sins described in great detail for all to read. But you will stand before the Lord one day. All of us will. Every knee will bow before God and every tongue will one day confess that Jesus is Lord (Romans 14:11). Perhaps the thought of standing before the Lord like that one day frightens you. Maybe you shudder at the thought of every day of your life being on display before the almighty and holy God.

Take heart! God has provided a way so that when you stand before Him, you can stand unashamed and totally free from any guilt. The step to take sounds too simple: like David, you must simply receive God's gift of forgiveness. Following the example of King David, pray as he prayed: "Have mercy on me, O God, according to your unfailing love" (Psalm 51:1 NIV). Then you can be confident that, regardless of your rap sheet, you are forgiven, and you can continue to follow David's lead spending the rest of your days on earth singing, "Let all that I am praise the LORD!" (Psalm 103:1).

Remember, God doesn't see people as celebrities or non-celebrities. "The LORD does not look at the things man looks at. Man looks at the outward appearance, but the LORD looks at the heart" (1 Samuel 16:7 NIV). He sees the hearts of His children and recognizes our need of a gift that only He can give. And He offers that gift to all of us. Forgiveness . . . for all.

ERIC

My name is Eric. Yes, the Eric from Renee's forgiveness story. I'm the one who took the life of her daughter Meagan and Meagan's best friend, Lisa.

I was a good kid. Twenty-four years old with a bright future ahead of me. But I single-handedly threw my whole life away. I made a decision that I thought wouldn't cause anybody any harm. I thought I could drive under the influence of alcohol one more time. I didn't mean to hurt anybody. I didn't think my actions would have any consequences. But this time my choice to drive drunk led to two beautiful young women losing their lives, and it landed me behind bars. It also led me into a deep depression that I never thought I would come out of. Here I was, twenty-four years old, and I had just been handed a sentence for almost as many years as I had been alive: I would spend the next twenty-two years of my life behind bars. My guilt felt like what I imagine Mount Everest looks like to an inexperienced climber: I never thought I would overcome it.

During my trial and sentencing, I was not a Christian. I had never thought I needed a savior. I was a scared young man, afraid of going to prison. It was hard for me to accept that I had killed two people. The attorneys had been telling me all along not to have any contact with the families and to stay distant. I knew in my heart it was wrong for me not to show any remorse. So, moments before the judge sentenced me, he asked if I had anything to say. I knew this was my chance to speak from my heart, so I did. It was so hard to look them in the eyes, but I needed to tell them how sorry I was. I told the families I would give my own life if it meant they could have their daughters back. I cried and cried as I tried to find the words to describe how sorry I was for what I had done.

July 29, 2003, is the day I accepted Christ. I was in jail and had talked with some of the other inmates about our situations. I was in a really bad place. The chaplain came by and told me that my mom had asked him to give me a Bible. His name was Chaplain Miller. I didn't really know anything about a personal relationship with Christ. But as the reality of prison sank in, I had lost all hope. I remember thinking, *At this moment, yeah, I do need a Savior.* So I talked to the chaplain, he prayed with me, and I accepted Christ into my heart.

When the forgiveness came, it was like I was pulled out from a deep, dark forest of despair. It was like being brought out of darkness and into the light. I get goose bumps when I talk about it. I felt like I could almost see the trees flying by as I was being pulled from this hopeless place in my life. It was the kind of relief that you feel when you think you're lost but all of a sudden realize that you know where you are. All of a sudden I knew where I was and who I was in Christ. I felt like the weight of the world had been taken off of me. I felt like God was saying to me, "You're not lost anymore. I've got you."

Now, here I am, and I've been given a second opportunity at life because of forgiveness. Renee chose to forgive me for taking the life of her daughter. I don't know how, but I am forever grateful that she has. Her whole family followed her lead. The family even went before a judge on my behalf and asked the judge to show leniency. Renee and nine of her family members each took turns speaking to the judge. I told my attorney that, regardless of the judge's decision that day, I had already received the blessing. Words cannot express how hearing them speak on my behalf healed my heart. The judge cut my sentence in half. After serving nine years and four months—or, as I look at it, three thousand four hundred eleven days—I am a free man in more ways than one. Thanks to Renee's forgiveness and, most importantly, to the grace that God has given to me, this prisoner has literally been set free!

Forgiveness means life to me. Without the forgiveness of Renee and her family, I would not only still be in prison, but I would also still be a very burdened person. I would still feel the hatred: I would know that I was hated. I would know that the two families still held resentment in their hearts, and that knowledge would have been so hard for me to deal with. And I have to be honest. I know the families have forgiven me. I know God has forgiven me. But, in my flesh, it is still really hard for me to believe that I am worthy of forgiveness. I know that thought is from the devil. That is why he is called a "worthy adversary." Because he will play tricks with me, saying things like, "Who are you to think that you can be forgiven for what you've done?" A lot of times I feel unworthy of forgiveness. But at the same time I am reminded that I have to forgive myself to completely embrace what this family and what God have done for me. So, on a daily basis, I have to remember I am a new creation and I'm forgiven for all the sins in my past. I am pressing on toward the mark, not getting lost in my past anymore. It is a constant process for me. I will always remember where I came from, but I don't dwell on it. What I do dwell on is the fact that I've been given a second chance. I've received undeserved mercy. And I have been given the opportunity now to be a witness of God's forgiveness to the whole world. To me, forgiveness is everything.

NOT GUILTY

"He himself bore our sins" in his body on the cross, so that we might die to sins and live for righteousness; "by his wounds you have been healed."

1 Peter 2:24 NIV

Go ahead. Take a moment to grab that tissue and dry your eyes. (If Eric's story moved your heart like it did mine, I'm willing to bet you'll need more than one.)

I can think of no clearer picture of the power of forgiveness than this story you just read: a prisoner found guilty, sentenced accordingly, paying the price for his mistakes, yet receiving a second chance at life and being set free by the undeserved gift of mercy.

I close my eyes and try to imagine the scene Eric described, that scene when Renee and her family stood before the judge to speak on behalf of this guilty prisoner. My heart is moved by this courtroom miracle:

First a mother who lost her daughter speaks to the judge.
Then a sister who will never see her twin again.
Then a heartbroken father who misses his little girl
    every day.
Then the older brother who always protected her and
    longed to protect her once more.

And on, and on, and on.
One by one, they each took the stand.
One wronged party after another. One wounded heart after another. Each one taking turns not to throw a stone, not to spew venomous words of revenge, not to seek justice. But instead, asking the judge to have mercy on Eric. And as each family member took a turn, I imagine Eric feeling his heart being slowly and gently sewn back together, stitch by stitch by stitch.

Did you know that Someone has done that for you too? Someone has gone before a Judge to speak on your behalf. You might wonder, *Why would someone need to do that for me*? Well, the Bible says that we are all prisoners. Oh, not all of us will know what it's like to be physically behind bars like Eric was. But all of us are prisoners, held captive by sin from the day we are born. According to the apostle Paul, "All have sinned and fall short of the glory of God" (Romans 3:23 NIV). Paul described himself as "a slave to the law of sin" (Romans 7:25 NIV). The Bible also makes us aware of the sobering consequences of our sin: "the wages of sin is death" (Romans 6:23). Yes, it would appear that our fate is sealed, the verdict is in, and each one of us has been found guilty. But I am so glad that the story does not end there!

As Jesus hung on the cross, nails pierced His hands and feet, blood flowed from His body, and He thought of you. He thought of me. Jesus was not just speaking of the Roman soldiers when He said, "Father, forgive them, for they don't know what they are doing" (Luke 23:34). Jesus stood before the ultimate Judge once and for all, and He spoke on your behalf. He spoke on my behalf. And, in response, the Judge graciously granted us leniency: "God demonstrates his own love for us in this: While we were still sinners, Christ died for us" (Romans 5:8 NIV). And because of His death, "there is now no condemnation for those who are in Christ Jesus" (Romans 8:1 NIV).

Eric's description of being pulled out of a dark forest made me think of these words penned by D. L. Moody: "A great many people want to bring their faith, their works, their good deeds to Him for salvation. Bring your sins, and He will bear them away into the wilderness of forgetfulness, and you will never see them again."[3] When God in His infinite grace brought Eric out from the darkness, one thing stayed behind. His sin. Eric's dark forest of despair had been transformed into a "wilderness of forgetfulness." The same can be true for you. You were never meant to stay a prisoner. Jesus spoke to the Judge on your behalf. The Judge has granted grace. God's forgiveness has set you free . . . once and for all.

Forgiveness

Show me how to finally set it free
Show me how to see what your mercy sees
Help me now to give what you gave to me

Forgiveness

BEST DAY EVER!

The other day, while my daughter and I were on a walk, I heard her shout these three little words: "BEST DAY EVER!!!" She had gone up ahead of me a ways so, naturally, I picked up my speed to find out what prompted her to make such a bold proclamation. "Why is it the best day ever, Lulu?" I asked. "Because I saw a puppy!" When you're seven years old, it doesn't take much to make an ordinary day extraordinary. You'd think something amazing must happen for a day to earn a title like that. Yet I hear these three words exclaimed quite often around our house. Delaney, my four-year-old daughter, gets to skip her afternoon nap because of a change of plans: "BEST DAY EVER!" The girls get a scoop of ice cream after dinner: "BEST DAY EVER!" We see a rainbow after a spring shower: "BEST DAY EVER!"

When we're kids, we are easily excited. As we get older, though, life has to work a little harder to prompt us to proclaim, "BEST DAY EVER!" My little girls' little catchphrase got me thinking about some of the best days of my life. I thought about the day that I graduated from college. (My mother said that was the greatest miracle she's ever seen.) That was a good day, as I held a diploma in my hand and walked down the aisle in my royal blue cap and gown. But the best day ever? No.

I remember my fourteenth birthday. My dad, my brothers, and I shared an equal passion for baseball, and being in Chicago, we were huge Cubs fans. I will never forget this particular birthday. My parents rented a limousine to drive us to Wrigley Field to see a ball game. Then, during the game, I saw my name on the scoreboard wishing me a happy birthday. That was a great day! Best day ever? Nope.

I think about May 10, 2003, the day that will forever go down as "Matthew West wins the lottery!" I don't know how it happened, but I got the most beautiful girl in Tennessee to walk down the aisle and say yes to this goofy kid who was way out of his league. That was an incredible day. But not the best day ever.

I think of two frigid winter days, one in January 2006 and the other in February 2009. Rushing to pack a suitcase. Driving like Earnhardt Jr. to get to the hospital. Not being able to feel my hand because Emily was squeezing it so hard. Hearing the doctor say, "It's a girl!" Those were two of my proudest days. Best day ever? Almost.

For all of the incredibly good days I've been blessed to experience in my life—and there have been many—only one can hold the distinction of "BEST DAY EVER." I was thirteen years old, a burned-out preacher's kid who spent almost every day of his life at church. Even at a young age, I had learned how to look and talk and act like I had this Christianity thing all together. I knew that if I raised my hand in worship at just the right time during a slow song, the old ladies seated behind me would whisper about how spiritual I was. I knew that if I sang a solo during the offertory, other parents would nudge their kids and say, "Why can't you be more like the pastor's son?" I knew that if I were polite to adults and stayed out of trouble, everyone would think I was a model Christian. But a personal relationship with Jesus? Well, I don't know that I really thought all that much about it. A relationship with Jesus just wasn't on my radar screen. I guess somewhere along the line I began to assume that I would get to heaven because I had connections. After all, my dad *was* a preacher, and I *was* a good kid. I should be covered, right? Well, little did I know that God was pursuing my heart: "Here I am! I stand at the door and knock" (Revelation 3:20 NIV).

One afternoon I settled down in our den with a bag of Cheetos and a remote control. There was a baseball game on, so my plans for the afternoon were set. But while I was flipping the channels, I stumbled across a different program, one I would usually be quick to skip past: a television evangelist preaching. Now you have to understand something about preachers' kids. Many of the TV evangelists made life at school hard for us. When kids would ask what our dad did for a living and I said that my dad was a preacher, the automatic response was "Oh, like those guys on TV who always ask for money?" Needless to say, I was quick to change the channel when I came across these types of programs. But this day was different. I had never really seen a Billy Graham Crusade before, and for some reason I couldn't bring myself to change the channel. Rev. Graham began to speak to thousands who were packed into a stadium, and I had a front-row seat right there in my living room. Everything he was saying I had heard a thousand times before, but it was as if it were the first time. My heart was pounding, and I knew something was going on inside of me that would change my life.

Rev. Graham was quoting Scriptures like "For all have sinned and fall short of the glory of God, and are justified freely by his grace through the redemption that came by Christ Jesus"

(Romans 3:23–24 NIV) and "For the wages of sin is death, but the gift of God is eternal life in Christ Jesus our Lord" (Romans 6:23 NIV). Again, these were Scriptures I had heard before, but the words resonated for the first time, and there was an undeniable stirring in my soul.

Well, right about that time, my mother, who is an amazing woman of prayer, happened to walk into the room. Startled, I'm sure, to see that I wasn't watching a baseball game, she quickly sensed that God was at work. She sat down on the couch next to me and asked me if I wanted to pray. I will never forget that moment. The choir on TV was singing "Just As I Am," and these words were hitting my heart in a real and powerful way:

> *Just as I am without one plea*
> *But that Thy blood was shed for me*
> *And that Thou bidst me come to Thee*
> *O Lamb of God I come, I come*

Then, just as Billy Graham was inviting people to invite Jesus into their hearts, a thirteen-year-old kid took his mom's hand and prayed a prayer that would change his life forever. Of all the days in my life—days past and those yet to come—I can say with great confidence that the day I found forgiveness was the BEST DAY EVER!

My dad always said that the day you accept Christ into your life is a memory you should always hold in your heart, just like you would keep a picture in your wallet. Well, I just shared my picture. What's yours? Have you ever acknowledged your own need for forgiveness? Have you experienced the freedom of new life in Christ? The journey we've taken together in this book and each of the stories you've read point to this most significant question: "Have you yourself received the gift of God's forgiveness?" No other question you ever answer will have a greater impact on the direction of your life.

What you choose to do about Jesus' invitation to receive the forgiveness He offers will also affect how you approach your relationship with others. Do you have to be a Christian to be able to forgive someone else? No, I'm not saying that. Can someone who doesn't know God resolve conflicts with others? Yes. But the truth is, apart from a personal relationship with Jesus Christ, our understanding of forgiveness can only go so far. The only way to fully comprehend how far forgiveness can reach is to know and believe in the One who reached the farthest: "God loved the world so much that he gave his one and only Son, so that everyone who believes in him will not perish but have eternal life" (John 3:16). This verse—the most widely known verse in the Bible—shows us the great lengths God was willing to go for the sake of forgiveness.

The verse that immediately follows is equally significant to our understanding of God's heart for us: "God sent his Son into the world not to judge the world, but to save the world through him" (John 3:17). God could have judged us, but instead He paid the price for our sins by sending His Son to die. God chose mercy over justice and has invited you and me to gather at His table of forgiveness just as the disciples sat with Jesus at the Last Supper. That is when Jesus offered His closest followers the cup and said, "Drink from it, all of you. This is my blood of the covenant, which is poured out for many for the forgiveness of sins" (Matthew 26:27–28 NIV).

C. S. Lewis wrote, "To be a Christian means to forgive the inexcusable because God has forgiven the inexcusable in you."[4] We can only extend forgiveness to the extent that we have received the forgiveness God extends to us. The greater our understanding of how much God has pardoned us for, the more willing to pardon others we will be. Over and over in the Bible, we are reminded that our forgiveness is closely connected to our need to forgive others and our ability to do so. In the Lord's Prayer, we learn to pray, "Forgive us our debts, as we also have forgiven our debtors" (Matthew 6:12 NIV). In His parable of the unmerciful servant, Jesus said, "Shouldn't you have had mercy on your fellow servant just as I had on you?" (Matthew 18:33 NIV). The servant had lost sight of the mercy his master had shown him, and as a result he failed to extend the same forgiveness to others.

The cup of forgiveness has been passed to you. Will you choose to drink from it? Are you ready to receive the forgiveness that has been poured out to you by a God who loves you with an everlasting love? The Bible says, "If you confess with your mouth, 'Jesus is Lord,' and believe in your heart that God raised him from the dead, you will be saved" (Romans 10:9 NIV). Maybe you have already prayed a prayer like the one below. Even so, I encourage you to pray this particular prayer with me as both a reaffirmation of your faith and a reminder of the forgiveness you have received:

Dear Jesus, I know I'm a sinner. I also know I can't make it through this life on my own. And I know that You died on a cross to pay the price for my sins. I ask You, right now, to come into my heart. Thank You for Your forgiveness and for the gift of eternal life. Help me to love others like You love me, and to forgive others as You have forgiven me. Amen.

"FORGIVENESS" SONG LYRICS

IT'S THE HARDEST THING TO GIVE AWAY
THE LAST THING ON YOUR MIND TODAY
IT ALWAYS GOES TO THOSE WHO DON'T DESERVE

IT'S THE OPPOSITE OF HOW YOU FEEL
WHEN THE PAIN THEY CAUSED IS JUST TOO REAL
TAKES EVERYTHING YOU HAVE TO SAY THE WORD
FORGIVENESS

SHOW ME HOW TO LOVE THE UNLOVABLE
SHOW ME HOW TO REACH THE UNREACHABLE
HELP ME NOW TO DO THE IMPOSSIBLE
FORGIVENESS

IT FLIES IN THE FACE OF ALL YOUR PRIDE
MOVES AWAY THE MAD INSIDE
IT'S ALWAYS ANGER'S OWN WORST ENEMY

EVEN WHEN THE JURY AND THE JUDGE
SAY YOU'VE GOT A RIGHT TO HOLD A GRUDGE
IT'S THE WHISPER IN YOUR EAR SAYING, "SET IT FREE"
FORGIVENESS

IT'LL CLEAR THE BITTERNESS AWAY
IT CAN EVEN SET A PRISONER FREE
THERE IS NO END TO WHAT ITS POWER CAN DO

SO LET IT GO AND BE AMAZED
BY WHAT YOU SEE THROUGH EYES OF GRACE
THE PRISONER THAT IT REALLY FREES IS YOU

SHOW ME HOW TO FINALLY SET IT FREE
SHOW ME HOW TO SEE WHAT YOUR MERCY SEES
HELP ME NOW TO GIVE WHAT YOU GAVE TO ME
FORGIVENESS[5]

ENDNOTES

INTRODUCTION
1. Philip Yancey, *What's So Amazing About Grace?* (Grand Rapids, MI: Zondervan, 1997), 93.

FORGIVING OTHERS
1. Lewis B. Smedes, *Forgive and Forget: Healing the Hurts We Don't Deserve* (New York: HarperCollins, 1996).
2. Corrie ten Boom, *Clippings from My Notebook* (Nashville, TN: Thomas Nelson, Inc., 1982).
3. Yancey, 98.
4. Lewis B. Smedes, *The Art of Forgiving: When You Need to Forgive, But Don't Know How* (Nashville, TN: Moorings, 1996), 27.
5. "Restored" words and music by Matthew West © 2012 Songs of Southside Independent Music Publishing, External Combustion Music and Songs for Delaney. All rights administered by Songs of Southside Independent Music Publishing. Used by Permission of Alfred Music Publishing, Co., Inc. All Rights Reserved.
6. Rick Warren, *The Purpose Driven Life: What on Earth Am I Here For?* (Grand Rapids, MI: Zondervan, 2002), 143.
7. William Arthur Ward, *Thoughts of a Christian Optimist: The Words of William Arthur Ward* (Anderson, SC: Droke House, 1968).
8. Elizabeth O'Connor, *Cry Pain, Cry Hope: Thresholds to Purpose* (Waco, TX: Word, 1987), 167.
9. Yancey, 11.
10. Harriett Beecher Stowe, *Uncle Tom's Cabin* (Boston, MA: Dana Estes & Company, 1902), 114.
11. Yancey.
12. Smedes, *Forgive and Forget*, 29.

ASKING FOR FORGIVENESS

1. Jenn Abelson, "Feuding over Friendly's: New England Ice Cream Institution Beset by Corporate, Sibling Rivalries," *Boston Globe*, March 18, 2007.
2. Martin Luther King Jr., *Strength to Love* (Minneapolis, MN: Fortress Press, 1977), 50–51.
3. Rose Fitzgerald Kennedy, *Times to Remember* (New York: Doubleday, 1995).
4. Anne Lamott, *Traveling Mercies: Some Thoughts on Faith* (New York: Anchor Books, 1999), 134.
5. "Love Stands Waiting" words and music by Matthew West © 2012 Songs of Southside Independent Music Publishing, External Combustion Music and Songs for Delaney. All rights administered by Songs of Southside Independent Music Publishing. Used by Permission of Alfred Music Publishing, Co., Inc. All Rights Reserved.
6. Based on the Twelve Steps of Alcoholics Anonymous, *The Big Book Online Fourth Edition* (Alcoholics Anonymous World Services, Inc., 2013).
7. Twelve Steps.

FORGIVING YOURSELF

1. C. S. Lewis, *Letters of C. S. Lewis* (Boston, MA: Houghton Mifflin Harcourt, 2003), 408.
2. Smedes, *The Art of Forgiving*, 171.
3. Max Lucado, *Just Like Jesus: Learning to Have a Heart Like His* (Nashville, TN: Thomas Nelson, 1998).

EMBRACING GOD'S FORGIVENESS

1. Frank Warren, *A Lifetime of Secrets: A PostSecret Book* (New York: William Morrow, 2007).
2. Brennan Manning, *The Ragamuffin Gospel* (Colorado Springs, CO: WaterBrook Multnomah, 1990).
3. Dwight Lyman Moody, *Great Joy, Sermons and Prayer-Meeting Talks*, rev. (Oxford, United Kingdom: Oxford University, 1883; digitized, 2006), 193.
4. C. S. Lewis, "On Forgiveness," in *The Weight of Glory and Other Addresses* (New York: Macmillan, 1980), 125.
5. "Forgiveness" words and music by Matthew West © 2012 Songs of Southside Independent Music Publishing, External Combustion Music and Songs for Delaney. All rights administered by Songs of Southside Independent Music Publishing. Used by Permission of Alfred Music Publishing, Co., Inc. All Rights Reserved.

Don't miss Matthew's newest albums, inspired by real life stories.

The Story of Your Life

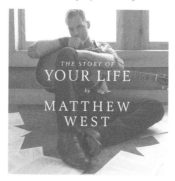

Features
"Strong Enough"
and
"The Story of Your Life"

Into the Light

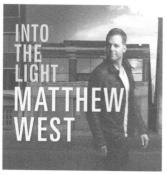

Features
"Hello, My Name Is"
and
"Forgiveness"

Available wherever you buy music
matthewwest.com

power

forgiveness

healing

joy

victory

for

restoration

victory

power

healing

forg

giveness

restoration

joy